HYMNS AND WED
FOR ALL HARPS

by SYLVIA WOODS

Each arranged for
beginning and advanced
harpers

A SYLVIA WOODS
MULTI-LEVEL
HARP BOOK

DEDICATION

This book is dedicated to all harp players who are making the festive occasions of life more beautiful by playing their music for others.

Cover Art by Steve Duglas
Music typeset by Robert Lau

Printed by Delta Lithograph, California, USA

All arrangements by Sylvia Woods

©1987 by Sylvia Woods, Woods Music and Books Publishing
P.O. Box 29521, Los Angeles, California 90029 USA

ISBN 0-936661-01-1

Table Of Contents

This is the third book in the SYLVIA WOODS MULTI-LEVEL HARP BOOK SERIES: books designed to be used by harpers and harpists of all levels of proficiency. Each tune has two arrangements: an easy version (A), and one that is more difficult (B). Also, each version contains chord indications that can be used by harpers or other instrumentalists.

Harpers and harpists can use this book in many ways, depending on their purposes and abilities. Here are a few suggestions.

1. A beginning player can play the melody alone, or with chords, or the complete easier arrangement.

2. More advanced players can play the easier arrangement, filling it out with more chords in the right or left hand, or play the second arrangement.

3. The easy arrangement can be played first, and then the harder arrangement, making a varied set.

4. The two arrangements can be played as a duet.

5. Additional instruments can be added to either arrangement, playing either the chords or the melody.

We hope you enjoy this book. If you'd like more information on other books in this series, and other books by Sylvia Woods, please write to Woods Music and Books, P.O. Box 29521, Los Angeles, CA 90029 USA.

INTRODUCTION

Some of my proudest moments are when I get letters from harp players all over the world saying that they have played some of my arrangements at church, a wedding, a party, or any other occasion. I think it is wonderful that harp players can share their gift and their talents with others, and bring even more joy to festive days.

I have received many requests from harp players for more music geared specifically to church services and weddings . . . two of our most popular performing venues. And that is the reason for this book. It contains hymns for church, and a variety of music for weddings of various faiths.

I hope that you and your harp will put this book to good use. Get out there and share your beautiful music with the world! I'm proud of you all!

With much love,
Sylvia

AMENS

Sometimes when you play the hymns in this book, you will want to add an "Amen". Just pick ONE of the "Amens" below that is in the correct key, and play it at the very end of the hymn.

For example, if the hymn is in the key of "C" or "A minor", (which means that there are no sharps in the key signature at the beginning of the piece), use one of the four Amens listed under "Key of C" below.

If the hymn is in the key of "G" or "E minor", (which means that there is one sharp in the key signature at the beginning of the piece), use any one of the three Amens listed under "Key of G" below.

It doesn't matter which Amen you pick as long as it is in the correct key. Try them all and see which one you thinks sounds best for each hymn.

Amens for Key of C

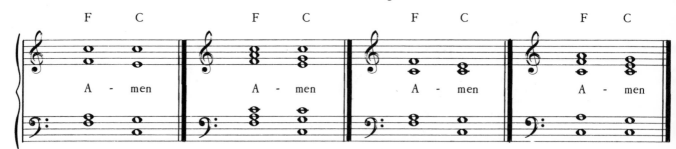

Amens for Key of G

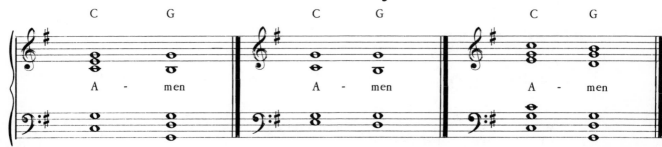

Many pieces from other books published by Woods Music and Books are appropriate for churches, weddings, funerals, and other events. This partial list will give you some ideas of pieces to try. These books can be ordered from Woods Music and Books, PO Box 29521, Los Angeles, CA 90029 or your local music store. The books listed here are:

"Teach Yourself to Play the Folk Harp" by Sylvia Woods
"40 O'Carolan Tunes for All Harps" by Sylvia Woods
"50 Christmas Carols for All Harps" by Sylvia Woods
"Irish Dance Tunes for All Harps" by Sylvia Woods
"Renaissance Music for the Harp" by Deborah Friou

FOR WEDDING PROCESSIONALS:
Lady Athenry (O'Carolan)
Carolan's Welcome (O'Carolan)
Morgan Magan (O'Carolan)
Captain Sudley (O'Carolan)
Hartes Ease (Renaissance)

FOR WEDDING RECESSIONALS:
Carolan's Concerto (O'Carolan)
Carolan's Receipt (O'Carolan)
Sir Charles Coote (O'Carolan)
Lady Gethin (O'Carolan)
La Volta (Renaissance)

INCIDENTAL WEDDING MUSIC:
Jesu, Joy of Man's Desiring (Teach Yourself)
New World Symphony (Teach Yourself)
St. Anthony's Chorale (Teach Yourself)
Wild Mountain Thyme (Teach Yourself)
My Love is Like a Red, Red Rose (Teach Yourself)
Greensleeves (Teach Yourself)
Greensleeves (Renaissance)
Corranto (Renaissance)

FOR FUNERALS:
Carolan's Farewell to Music (O'Carolan)
Carolan's Welcome (O'Carolan)
Bridget Cruise (O'Carolan)
Lord Galway's Lamentation (O'Carolan)
Blind Mary (O'Carolan)
Eleanor Plunkett (O'Carolan)
The Parting Glass (Irish Dance Tunes)
Carrickfergus (Irish Dance Tunes)
Farewell (Teach Yourself)
Jesu, Joy of Man's Desiring (Teach Yourself)
New World Symphony (Teach Yourself)
St Anthony's Chorale (Teach Yourself)

FOR CHURCH SERVICES:
Jesu, Joy of Man's Desiring (Teach Yourself)
O Sanctissima (Christmas Carols)
Let All Mortal Flesh Keep Silence (Christmas Carols)

Abide With Me

Moderately

music by W. H. Monk

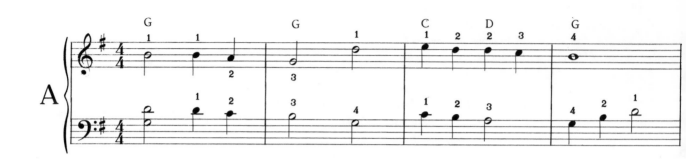

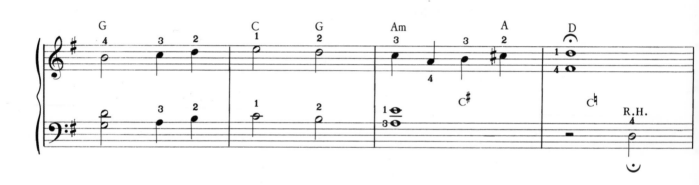

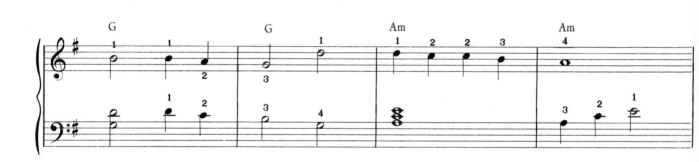

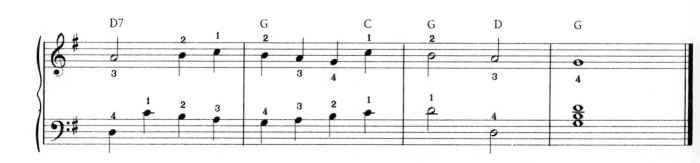

Abide With Me

Moderately

music by W. H. Monk

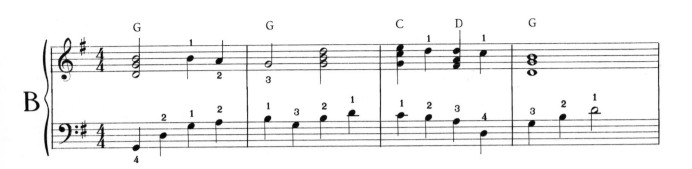

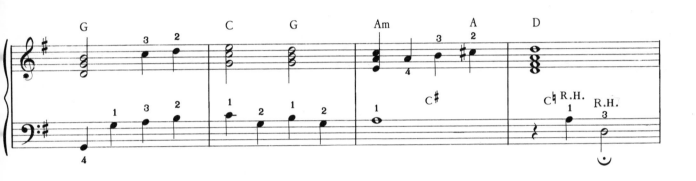

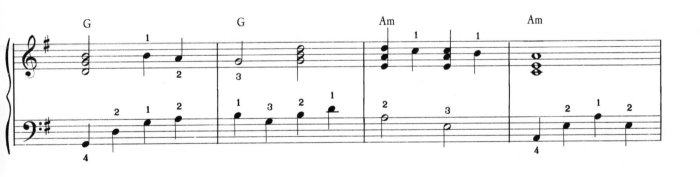

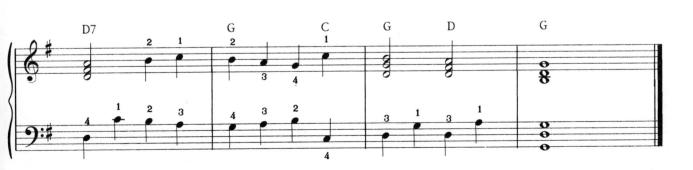

7

All Glory, Laud, And Honor

Majestically

music by Melchior Teschner

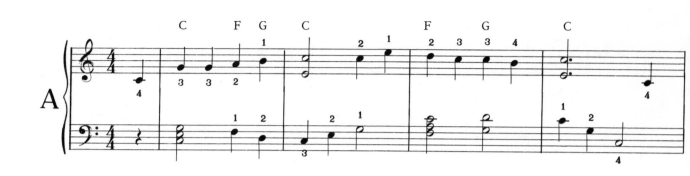

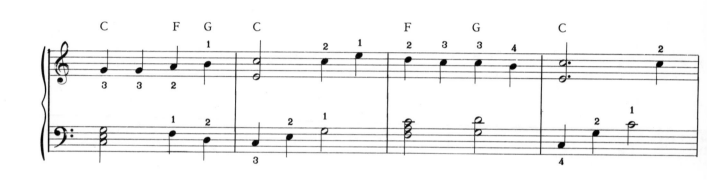

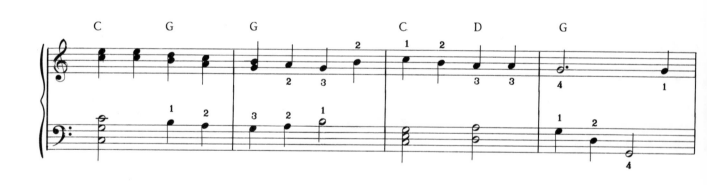

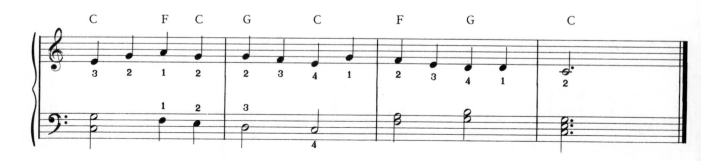

All Glory, Laud, And Honor

Majestically

music by Melchior Teschner

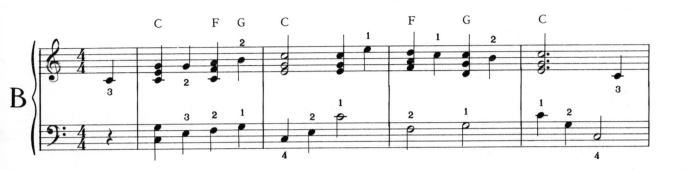

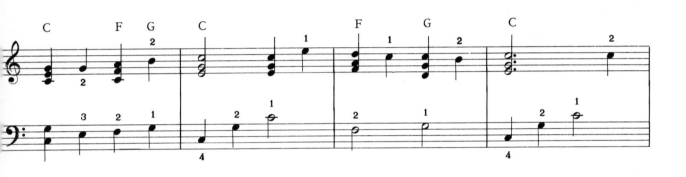

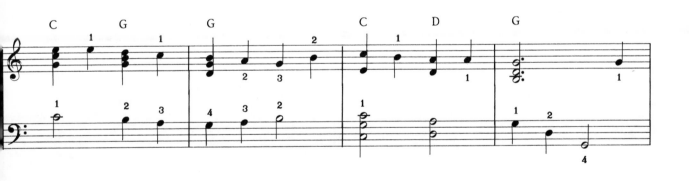

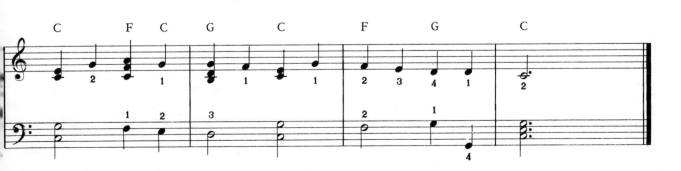

All Hail The Power Of Jesus' Name

Majestically

music by Oliver Holden

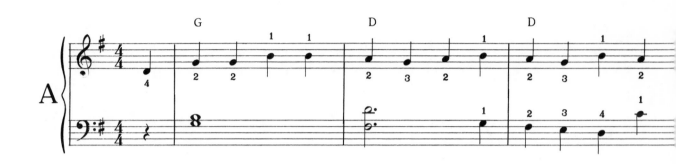

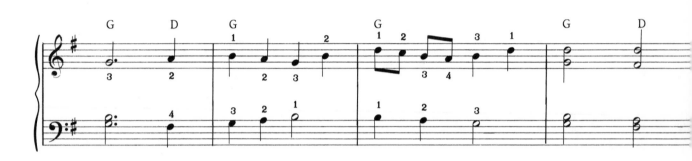

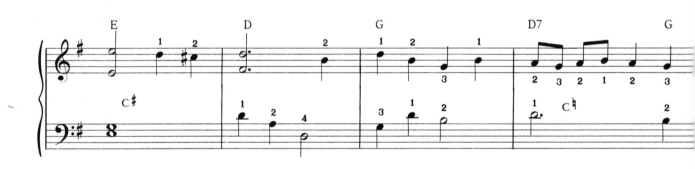

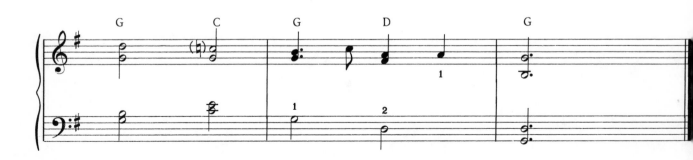

All Hail The Power Of Jesus' Name

Majestically

music by Oliver Holden

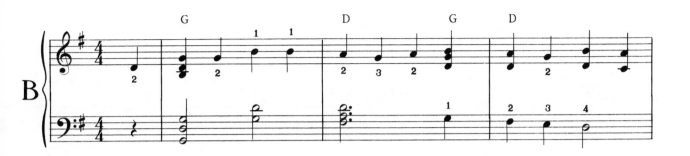

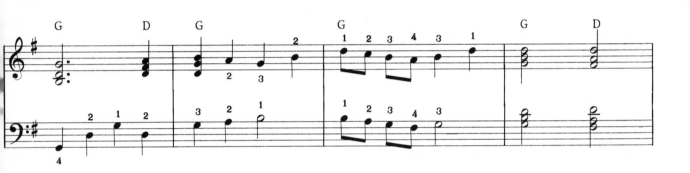

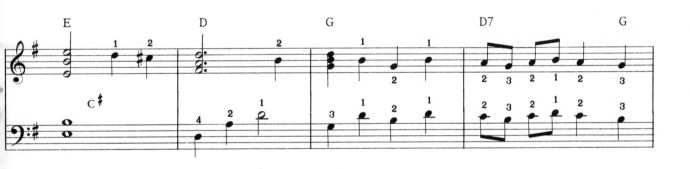

11

Amazing Grace

Flowing

American Folk Melody

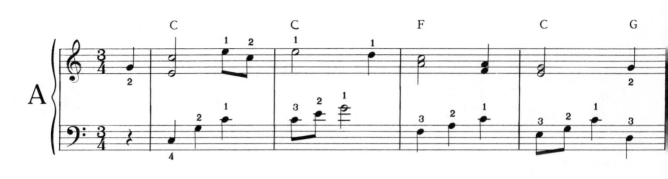

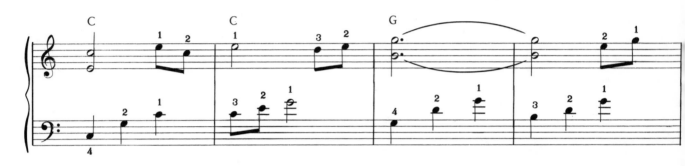

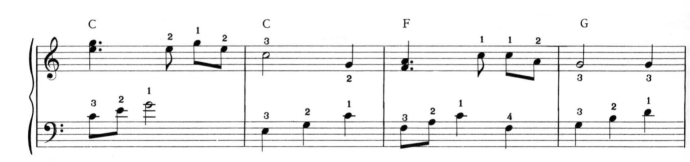

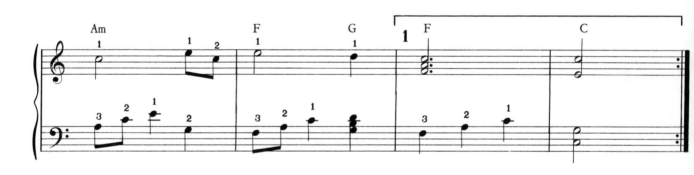

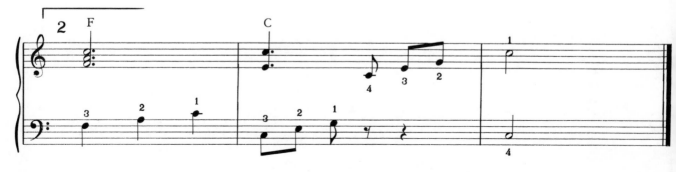

Amazing Grace

Flowing

American Folk Melody

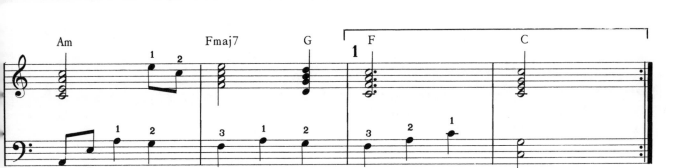

Be Thou My Vision

Moderately

old Irish melody

A

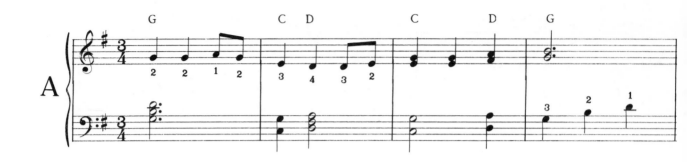

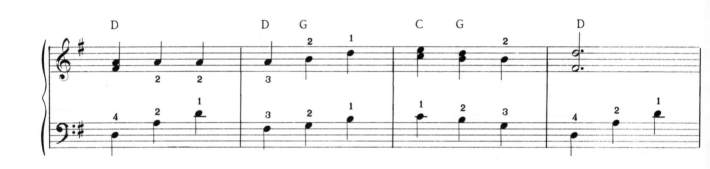

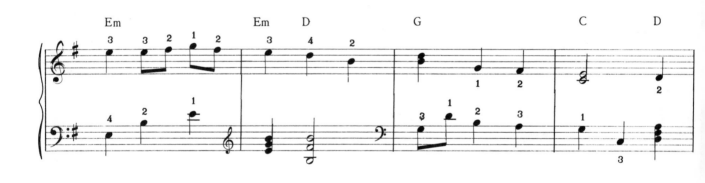

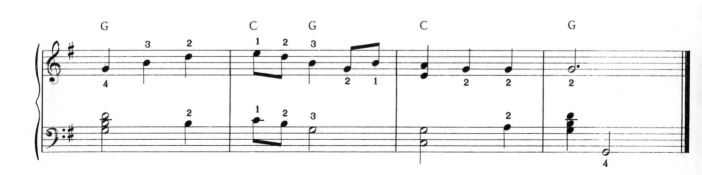

Be Thou My Vision

Moderately

old Irish melody

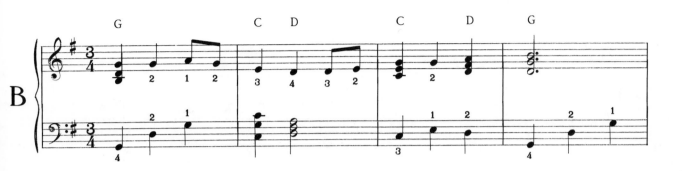

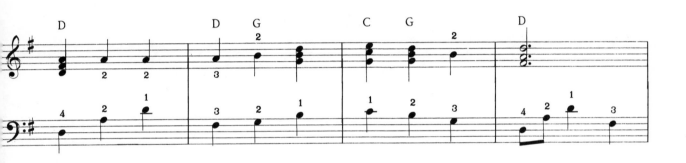

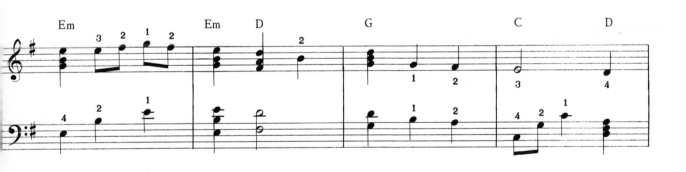

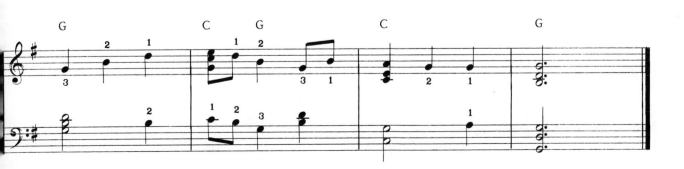

Blest Be The Tie That Binds

Moderately

music by Hans G. Naegeli

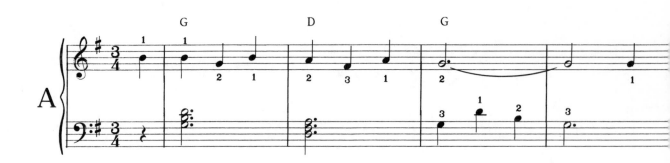

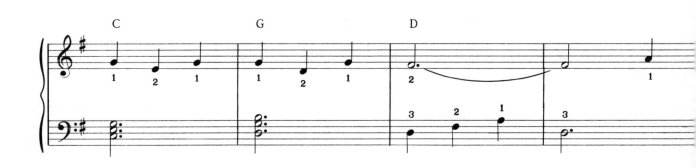

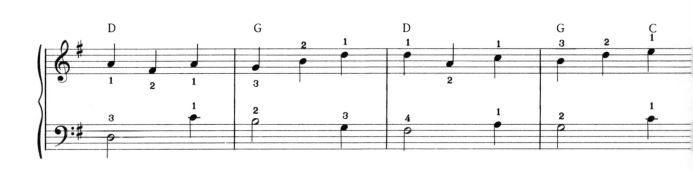

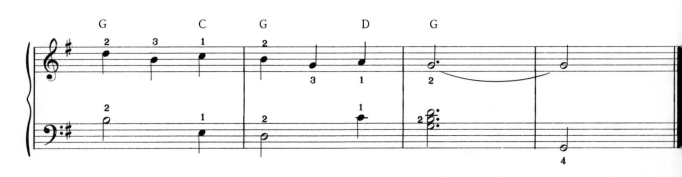

16

Blest Be The Tie That Binds

Moderately

music by Hans G. Naegeli

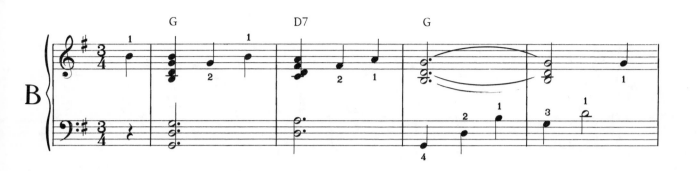

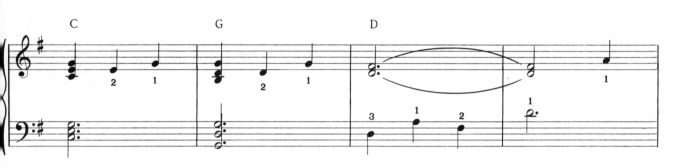

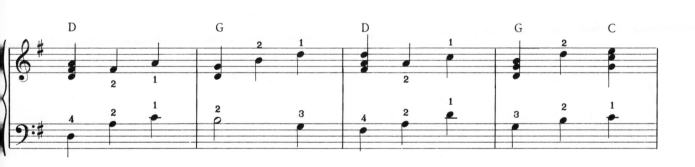

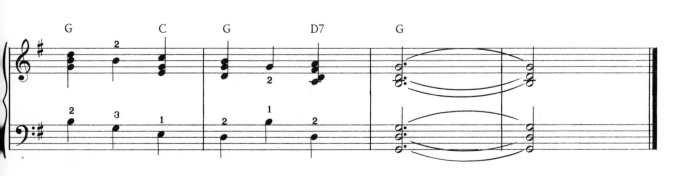

Christ The Lord Is Risen Today
Jesus Christ is Risen Today

Joyfully

music from Lyra Davidica

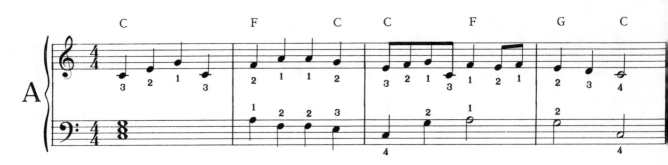

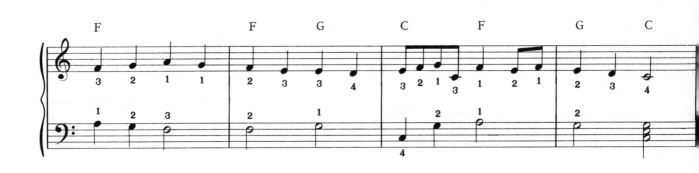

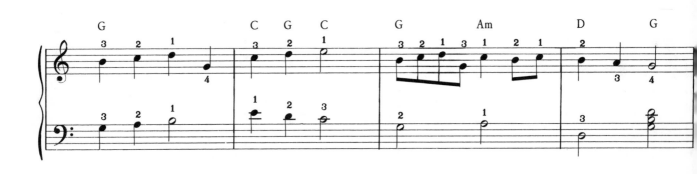

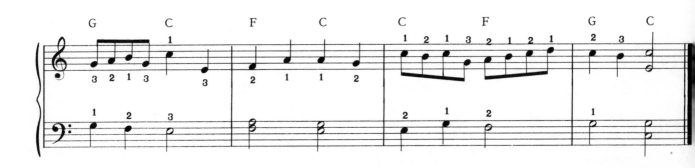

Christ The Lord Is Risen Today
Jesus Christ is Risen Today

Joyfully

music from Lyra Davidica

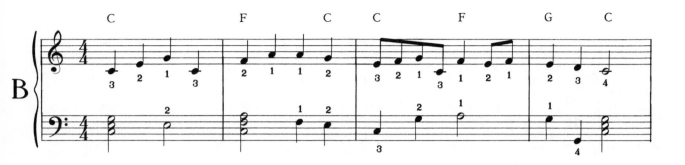

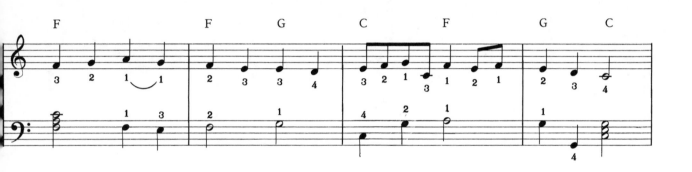

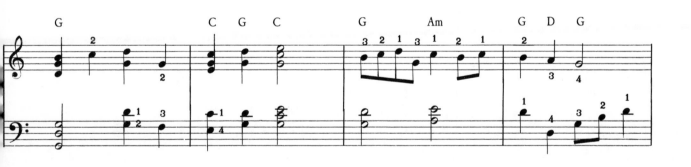

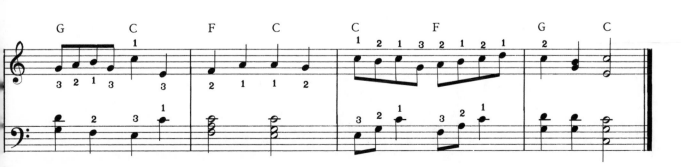

The Church's One Foundation

Moderately

music by Samuel S. Wesley

A

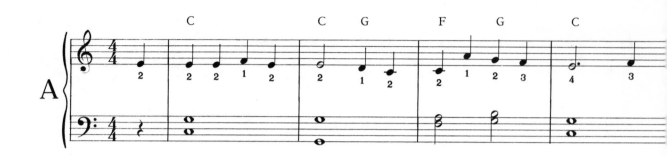

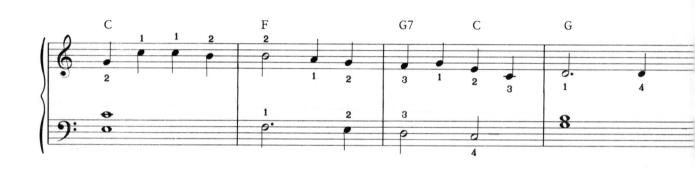

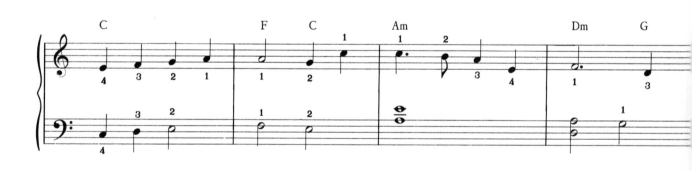

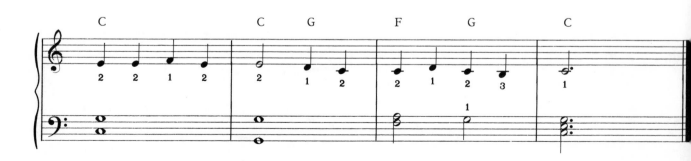

The Church's One Foundation

Moderately

music by Samuel S. Wesley

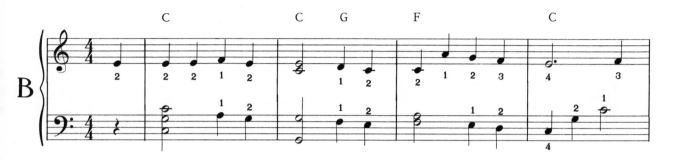

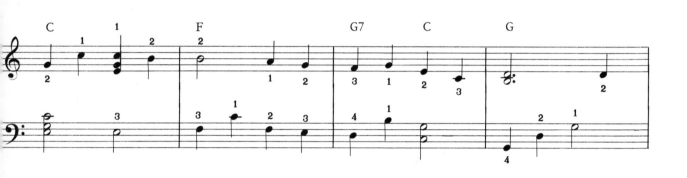

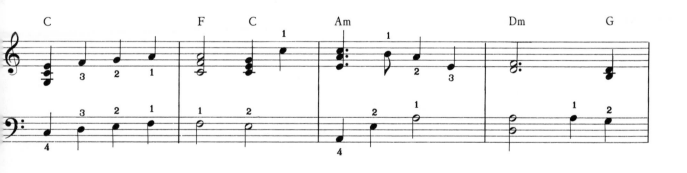

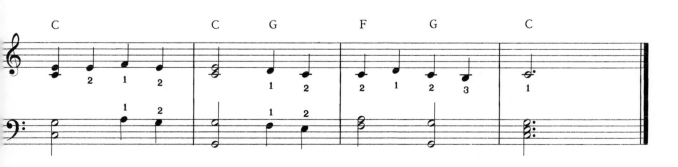

Come, Christians, Join To Sing

Joyfully

Ancient Spanish melody

Come, Christians, Join To Sing

Joyfully

Ancient Spanish melody

23

Come, Thou Almighty King

Stately

music by Felice de Giardini

A

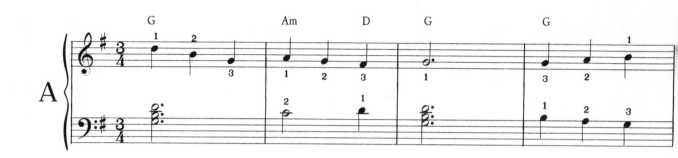

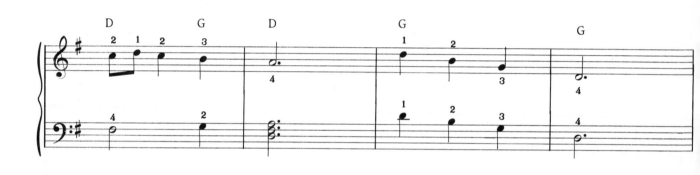

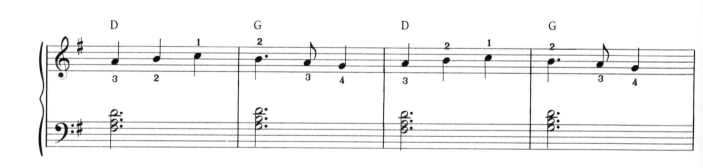

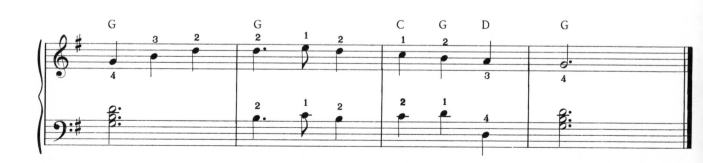

Come, Thou Almighty King

Stately

music by Felice de Giardini

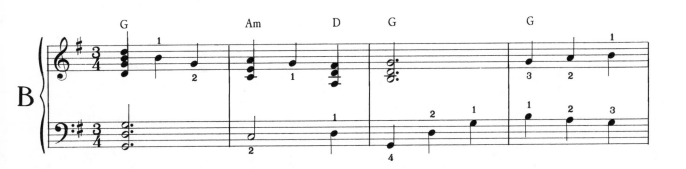

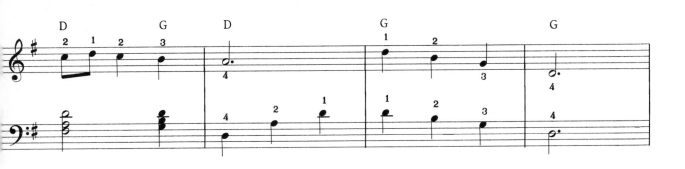

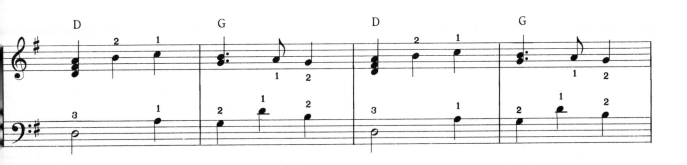

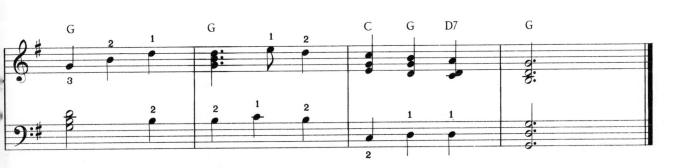

25

Doxology

Flowing

tune: Old Hundredth (Altered Rhythm)
music by Louis Bourgeois

All People That On Earth Do Dwell

Moderately

tune: Old Hundreth
music by Louis Bourgeois

Fairest Lord Jesus
Crusaders' Hymn

Moderately

Silesian Folk Song

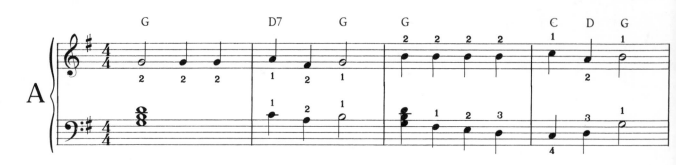

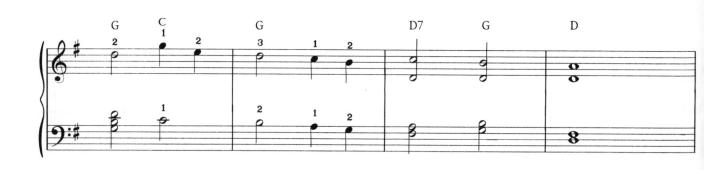

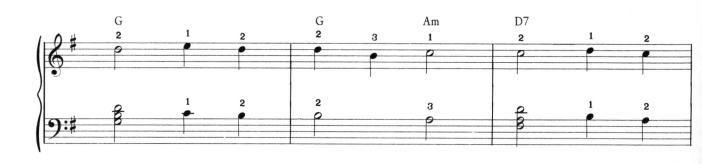

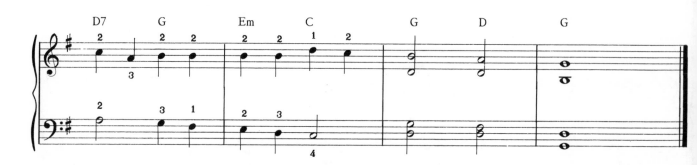

Fairest Lord Jesus
Crusaders' Hymn

Moderately

Silesian Folk Song

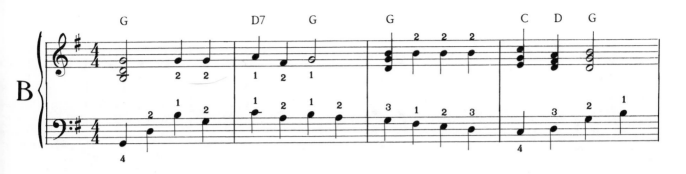

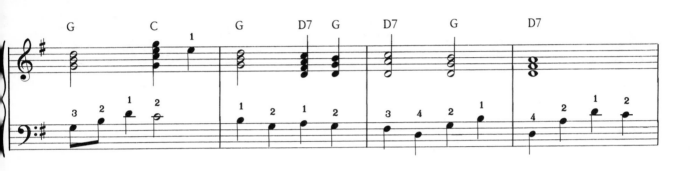

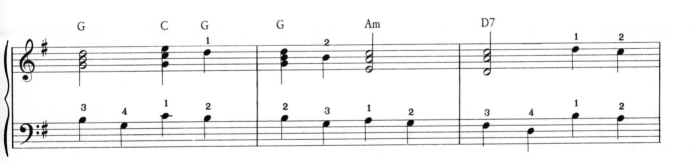

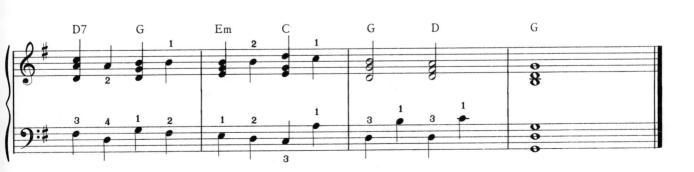

29

Faith Of Our Fathers

Moderately

music by Henri F. Hemy

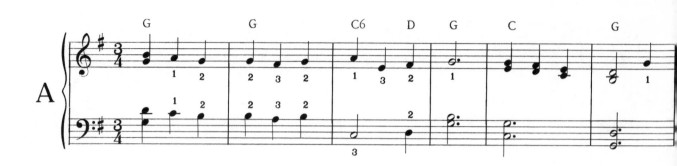

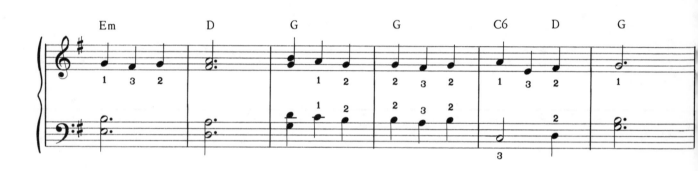

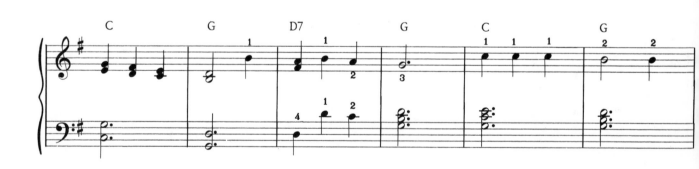

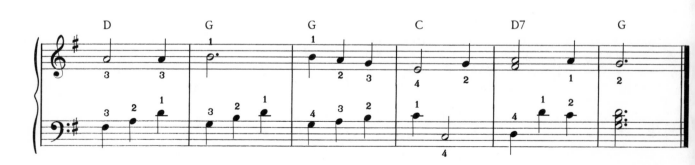

Faith Of Our Fathers

Moderately

music by Henri F. Hemy

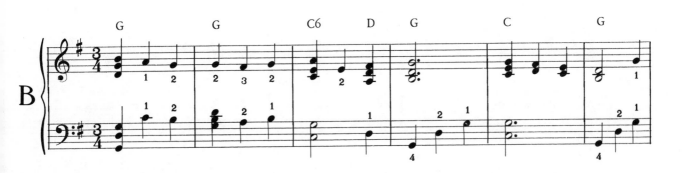

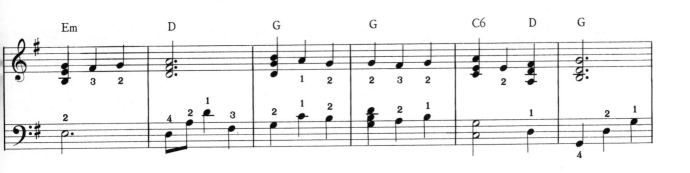

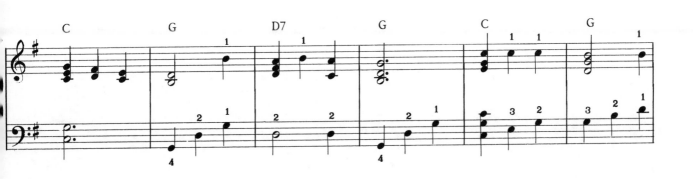

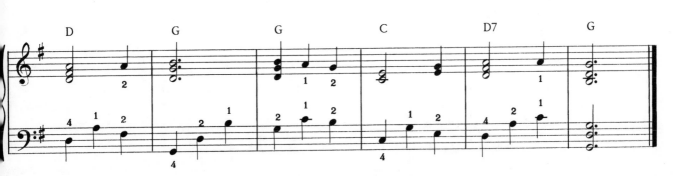

31

For The Beauty Of The Earth
As With Gladness Men of Old

Moderately

music by Conrad Kocher

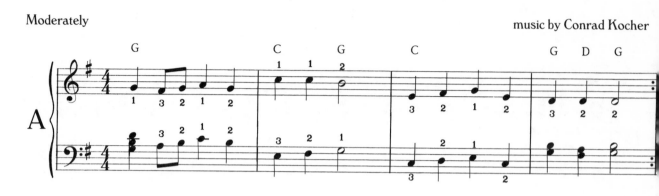

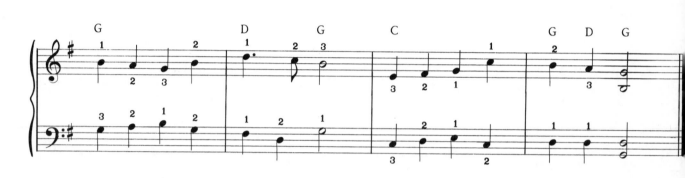

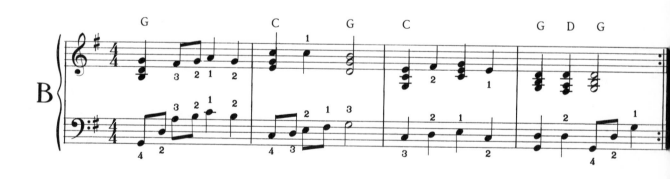

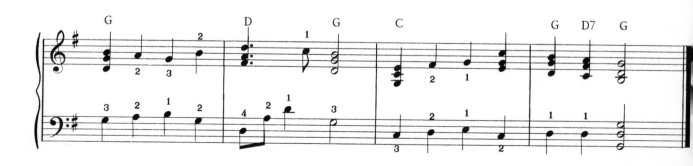

I Love Thy Kingdom, Lord

Moderately

music by A. Williams

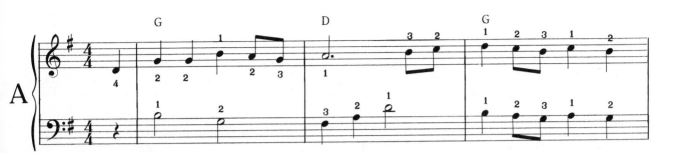

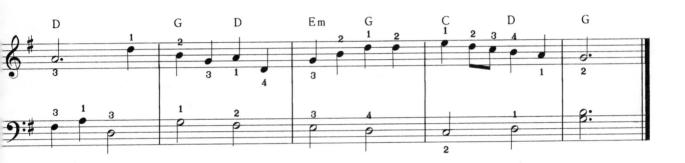

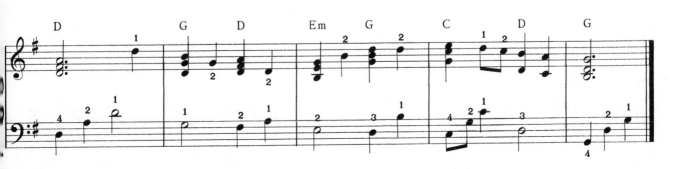

Guide Me, O Thou Great Jehovah

Majestically

music by J. Hughes

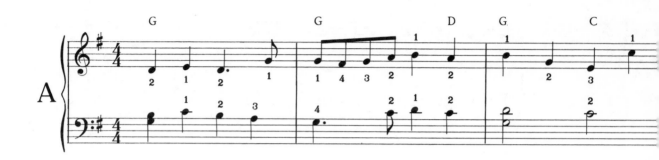

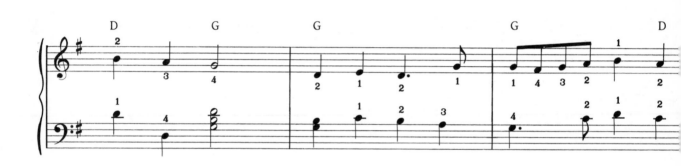

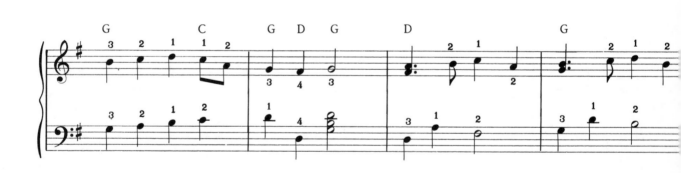

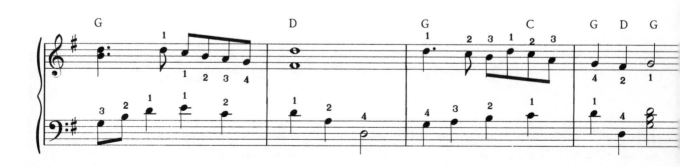

34

Guide Me, O Thou Great Jehovah

Majestically

music by J. Hughes

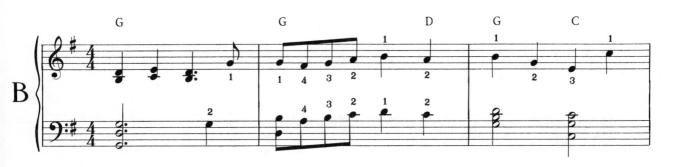

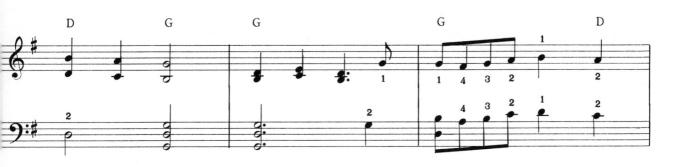

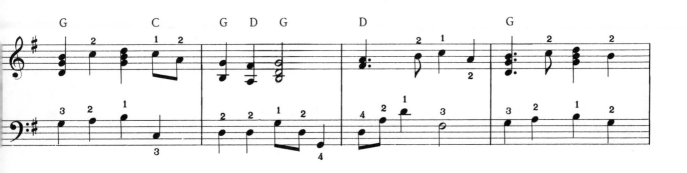

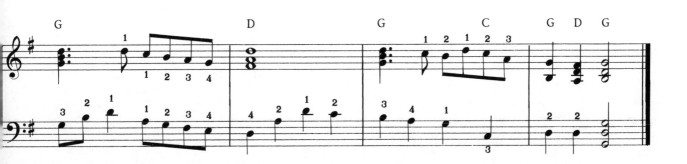

Holy, Holy, Holy, Lord God Almighty

Moderately and happily

music by John B. Dykes

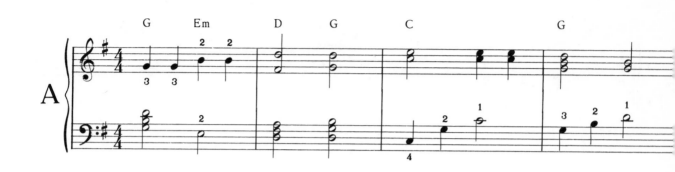

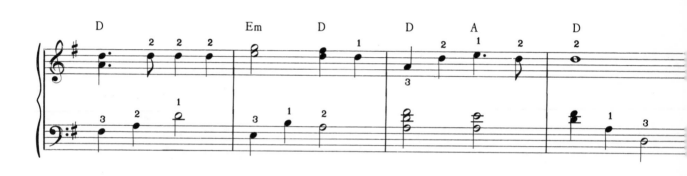

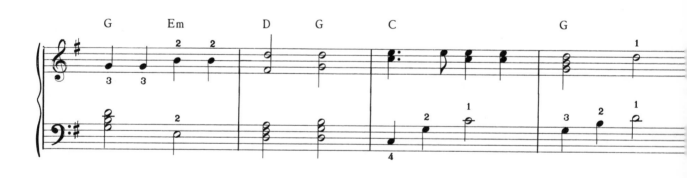

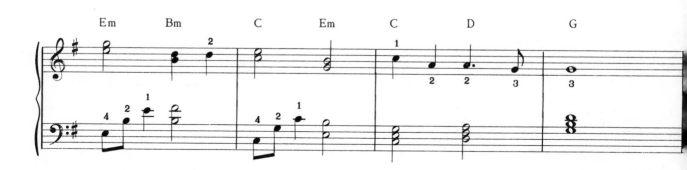

Holy, Holy, Holy, Lord God Almighty

Moderately and happily

music by John B. Dykes

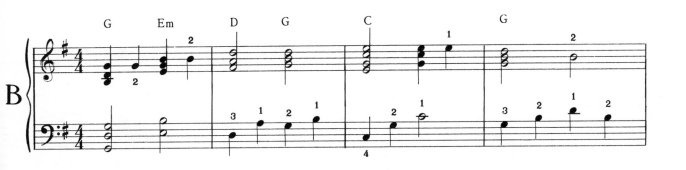

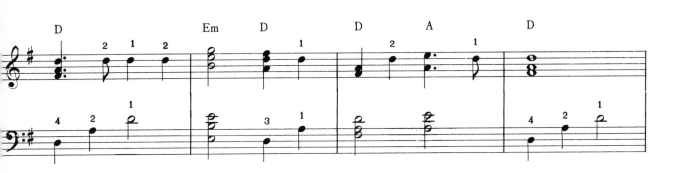

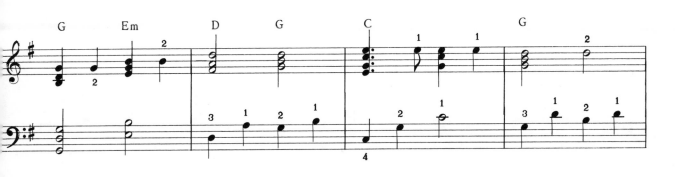

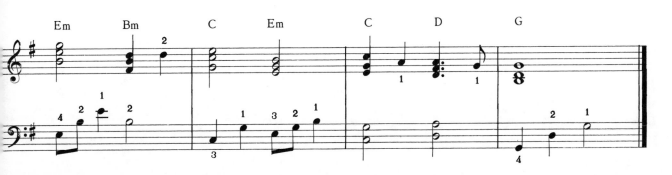

Jacob's Ladder

Folk harpers: Set the F an-octave-and-a-half above middle C as an F natural. All other F's should be set sharp. They will not change throughout the piece.

Slowly

Negro Spiritual

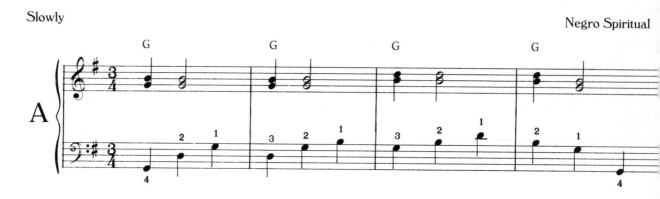

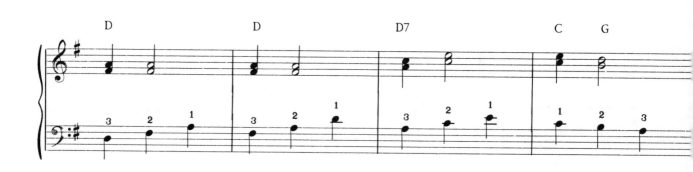

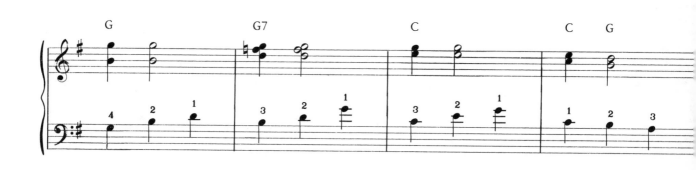

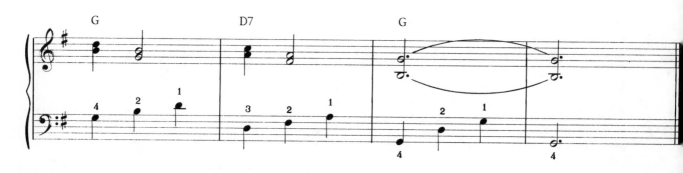

Jacob's Ladder

Folk harpers: Set the F an-octave-and-a-half above middle C as an F natural. All other F's should be set sharp. They will not change throughout the piece.

Slowly

Negro Spiritual

Jesus Loves Me

Simply

music by William B. Bradbury

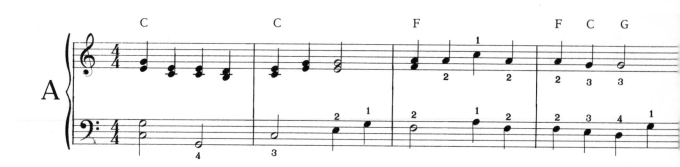

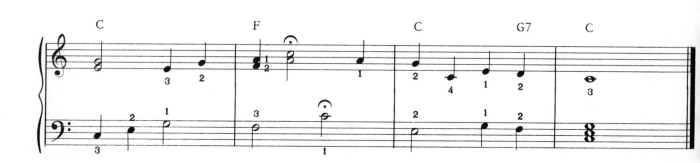

Jesus Loves Me

Simply

music by William B. Bradbury

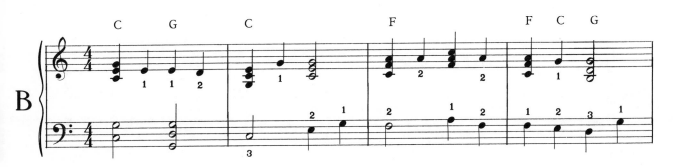

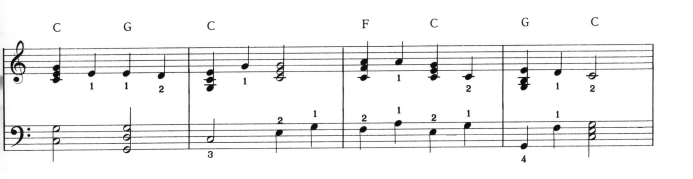

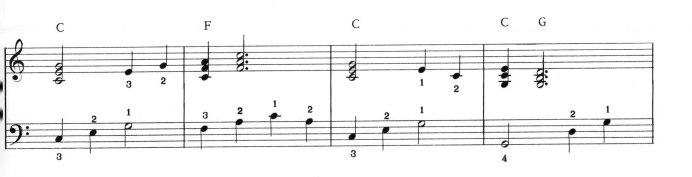

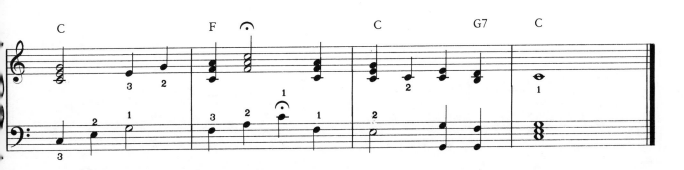

41

Kum Ba Yah

Flowing Traditional Nigerian

A

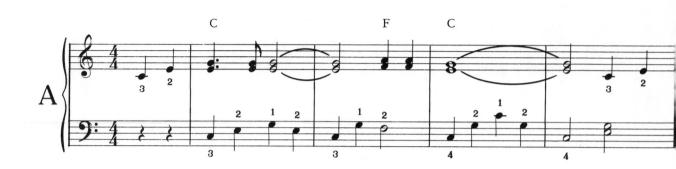

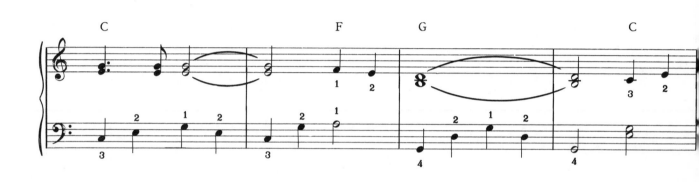

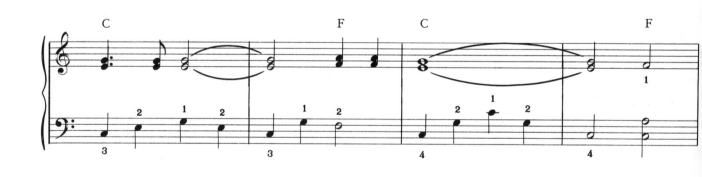

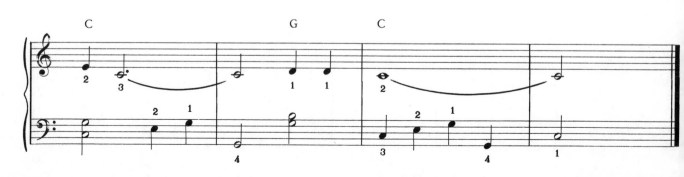

Kum Ba Yah

Flowing

Traditional Nigerian

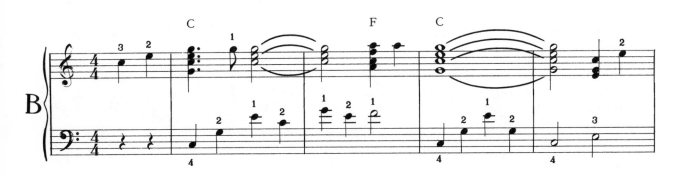

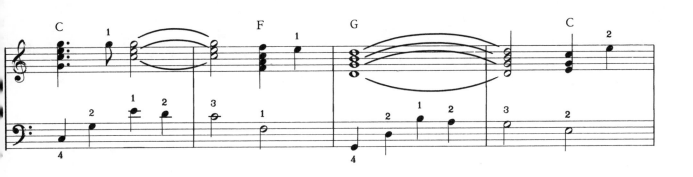

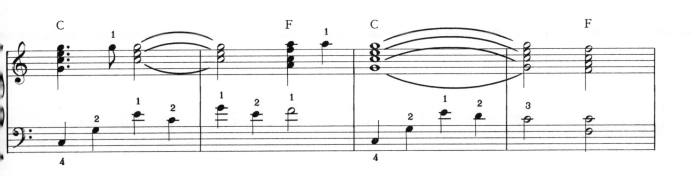

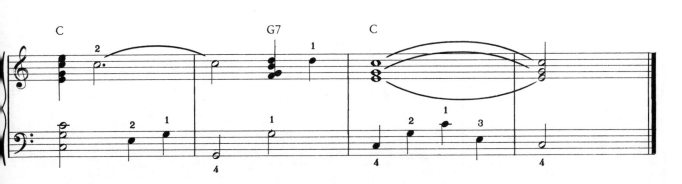

A Mighty Fortress Is Our God

Majestically

music by Martin Luther

A Mighty Fortress Is Our God

Majestically

music by Martin Luther

Morning Has Broken

Flowing

Traditional Gaelic melody

Morning Has Broken

Flowing

Traditional Gaelic melody

Nearer, My God, To Thee

Moderately

music by Lowell Mason

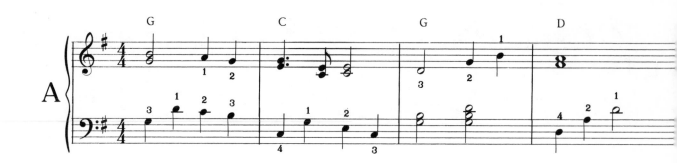

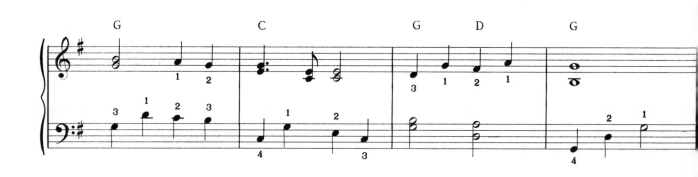

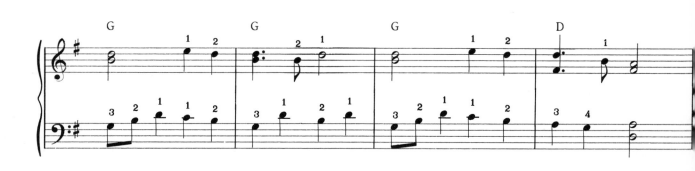

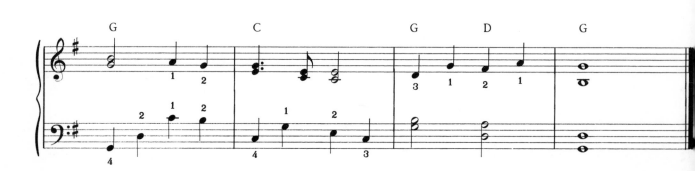

Nearer, My God, To Thee

Moderately

music by Lowell Mason

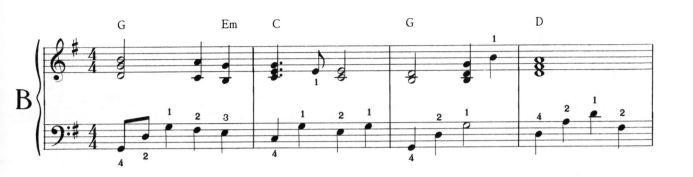

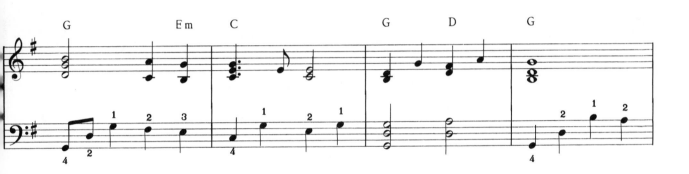

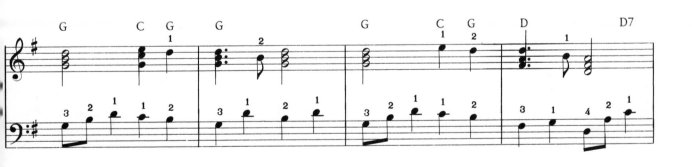

Now The Day Is Over

Flowing

music by Joesph Barnby

A
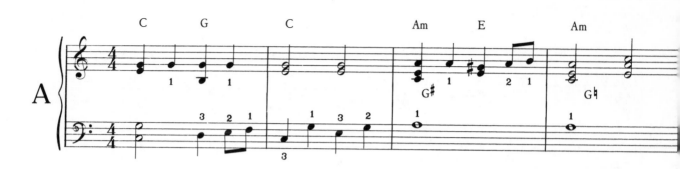

B
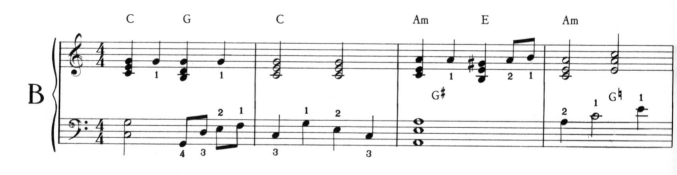

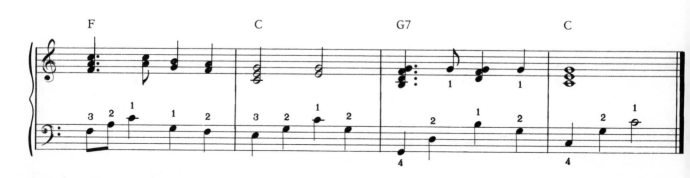

O God, Our Help In Ages Past

Folk Harpers: Set the F above middle C as an F sharp. All other F's should be natural. They will not change throughout the piece.

Majestically

music by William Croft

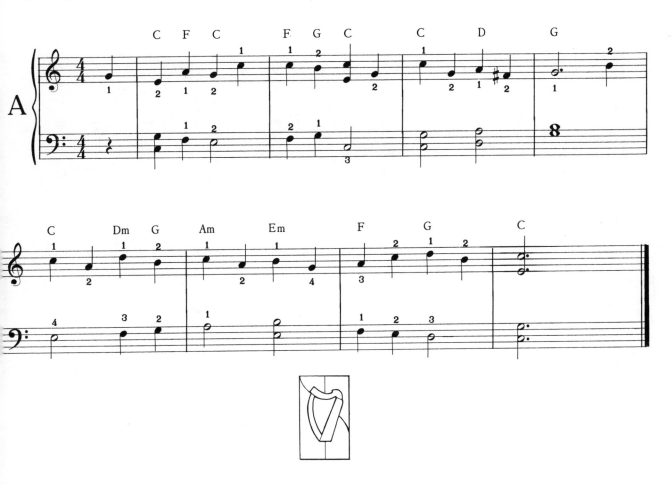

Folk Harpers: Set the F above middle C as an F sharp. All other F's should be natural. They will not change throughout the piece.

O Perfect Love

Flowing

music by Joseph Barnby

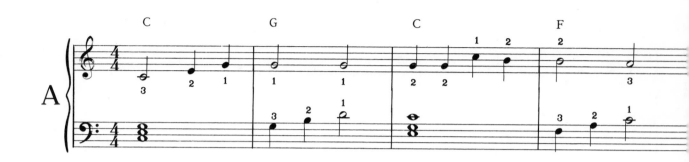

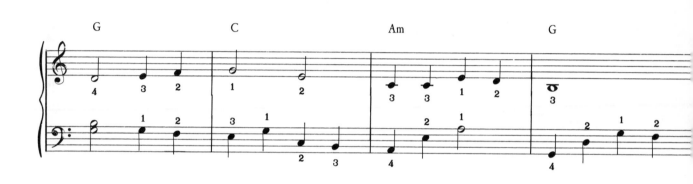

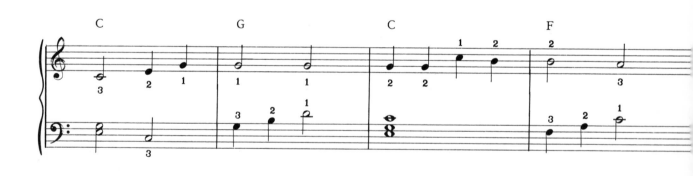

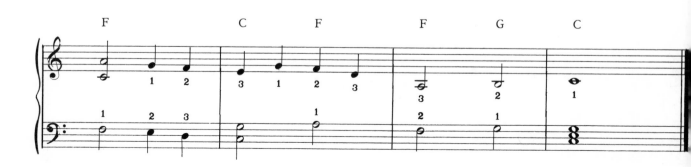

O Perfect Love

Flowing

music by Joseph Barnby

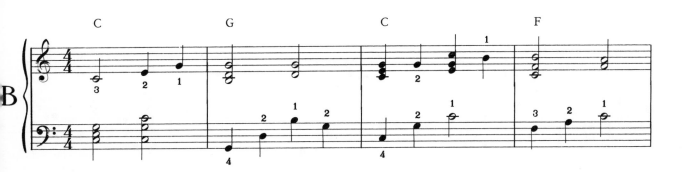

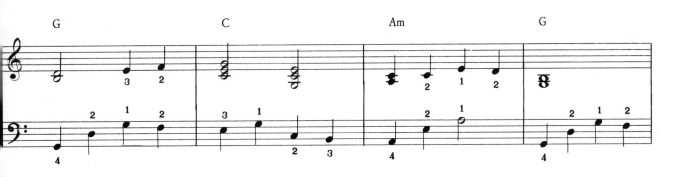

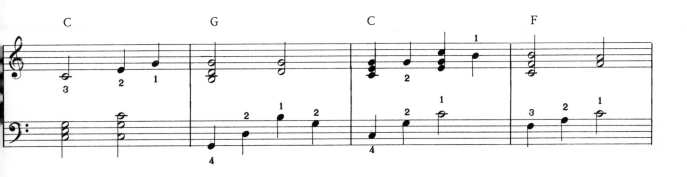

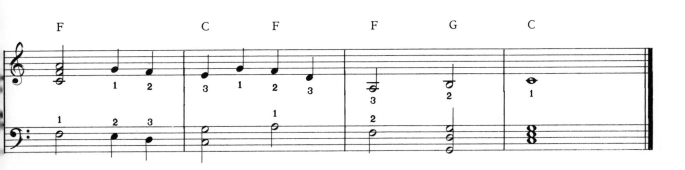

Rock Of Ages

Moderately

music by Thomas Hastings

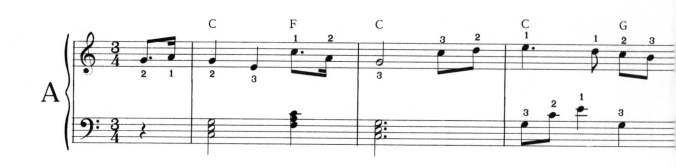

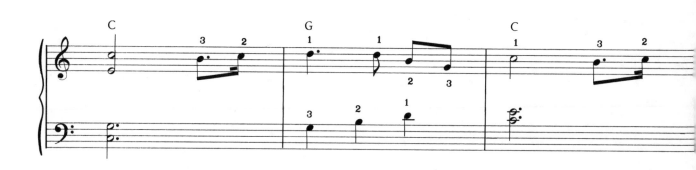

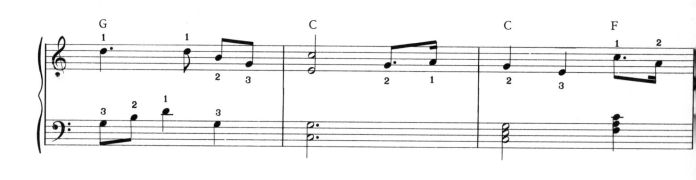

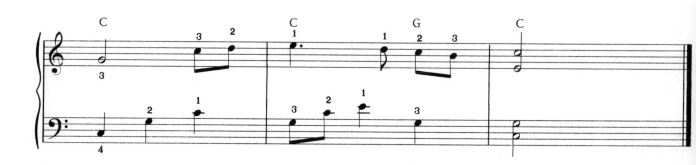

Rock Of Ages

Moderately

music by Thomas Hastings

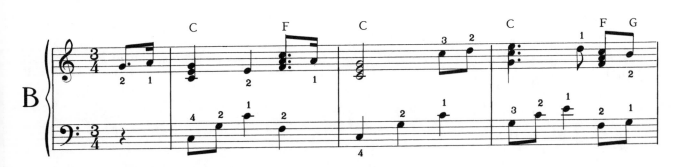

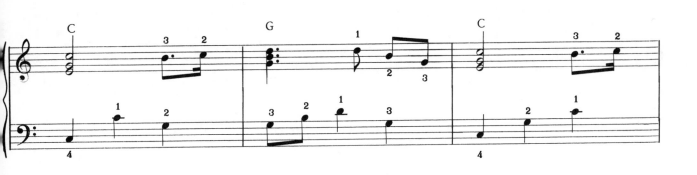

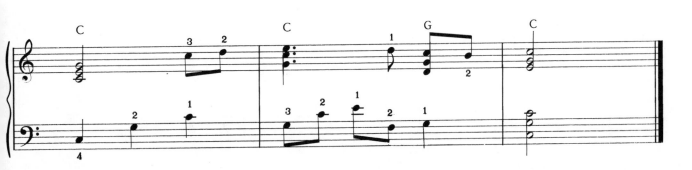

55

Stand Up, Stand Up For Jesus

Joyfully

music by George J. Webb

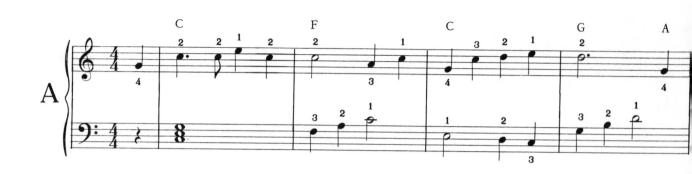

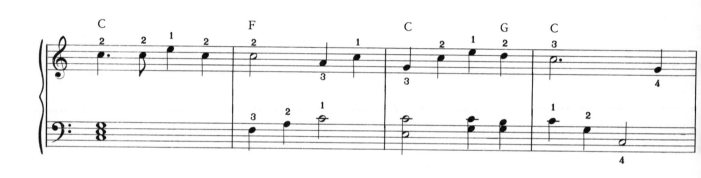

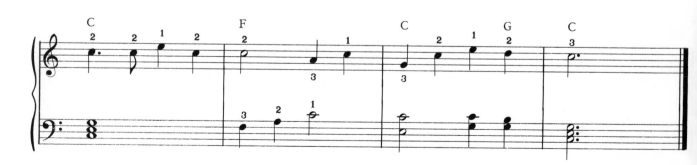

Stand Up, Stand Up For Jesus

Joyfully

music by George J. Webb

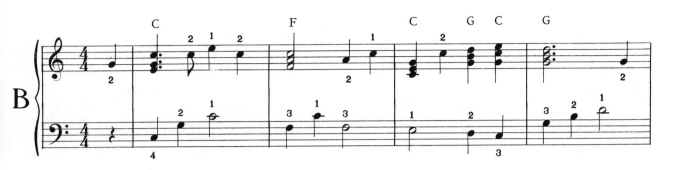

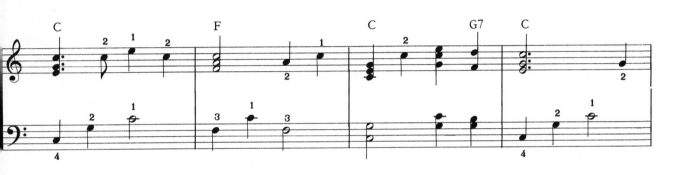

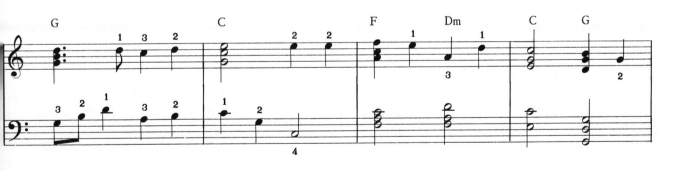

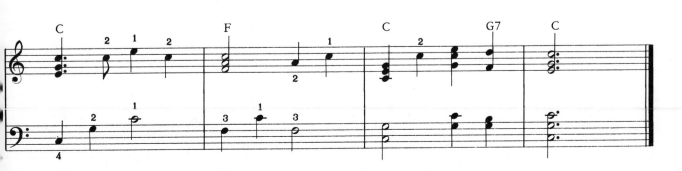

This Is My Father's World

Flowing

Traditional English Melody

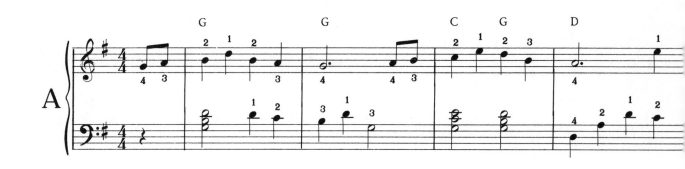

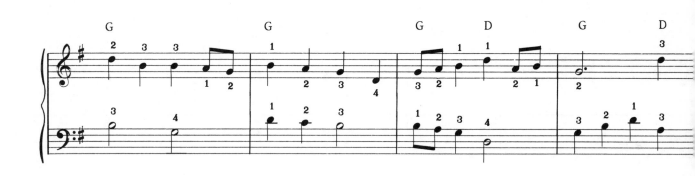

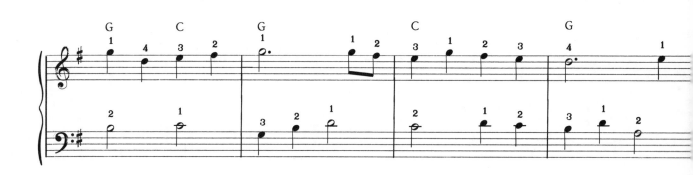

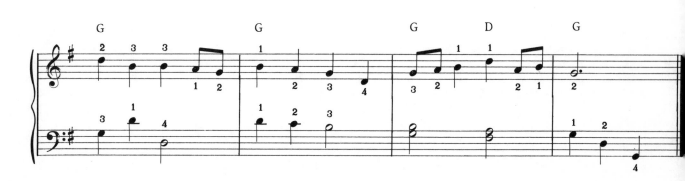

This Is My Father's World

Flowing

Traditional English Melody

B

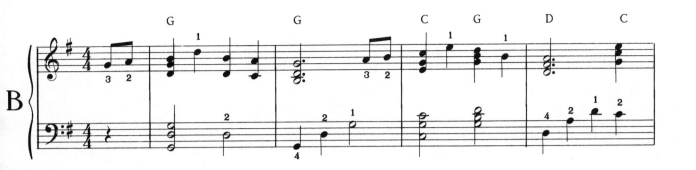

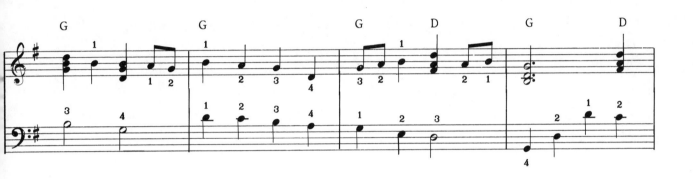

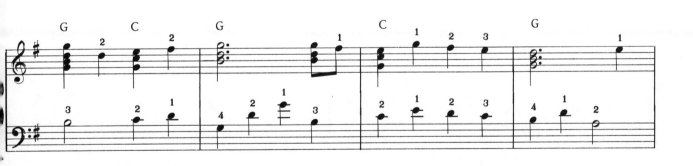

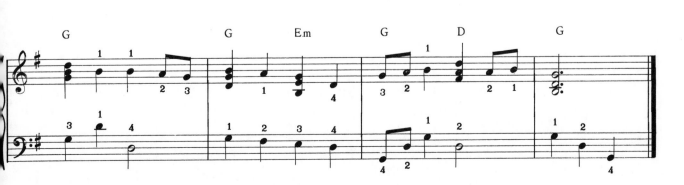

59

We Gather Together
Prayer of Thanksgiving

Moderately

traditional Netherlands tune

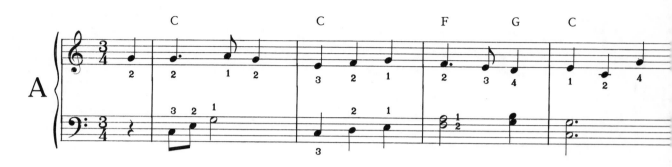

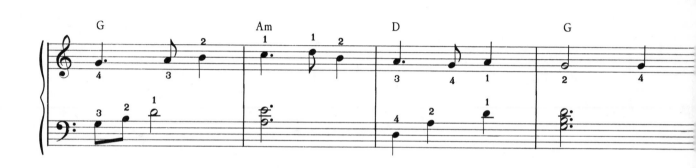

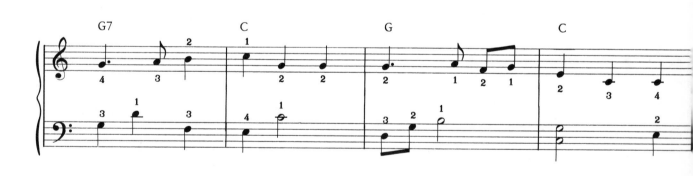

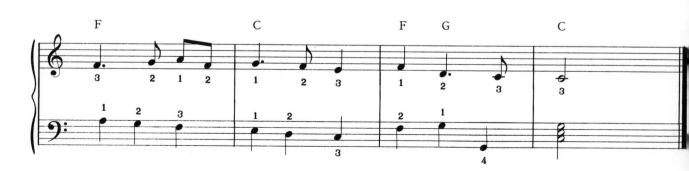

We Gather Together
Prayer of Thanksgiving

Moderately

traditional Netherlands tune

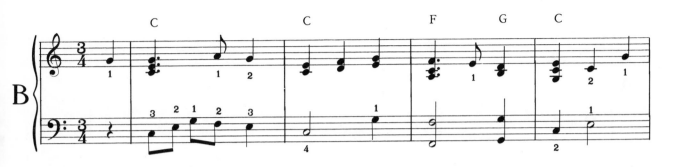

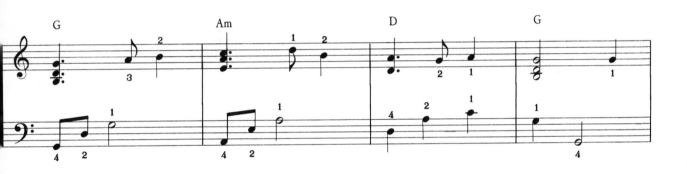

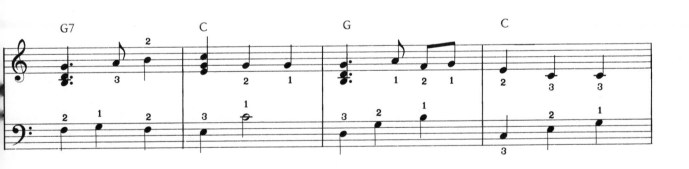

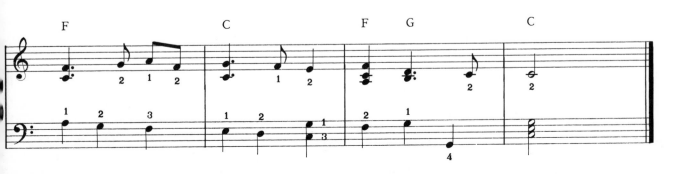

What A Friend We Have In Jesus

Joyfully

music by Charles Crozat Converse

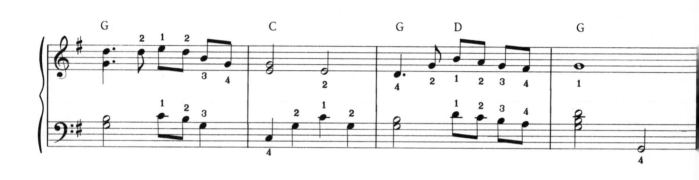

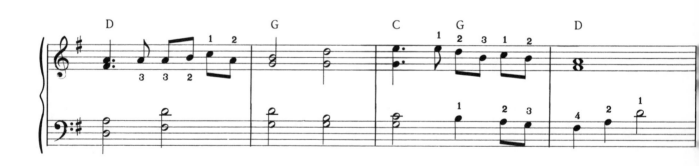

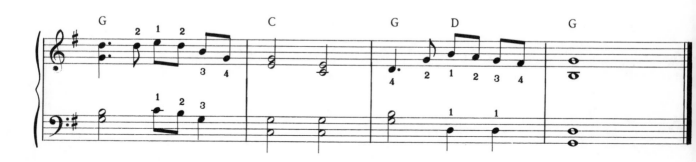

What A Friend We Have In Jesus

Joyfully

music by Charles Crozat Converse

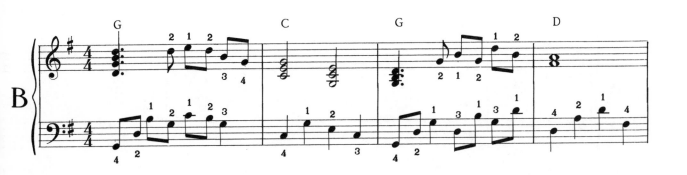

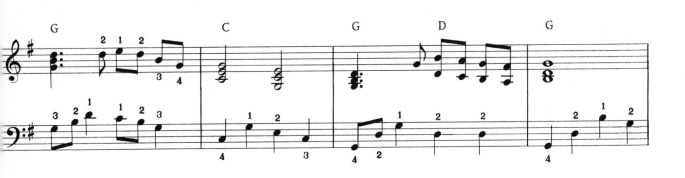

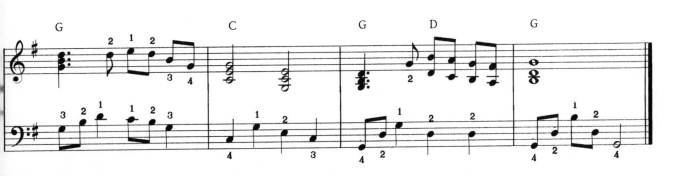

When Morning Gilds The Skies

Flowing

music by Joseph Barnby

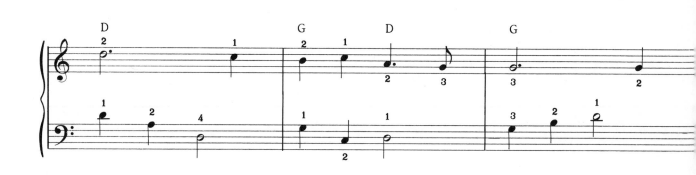

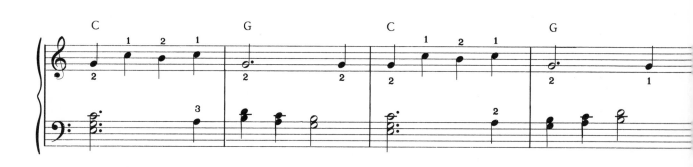

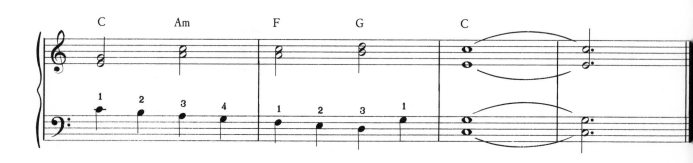

When Morning Gilds The Skies

Flowing

music by Joseph Barnby

Folk harpers: Set the F below middle C as an F sharp.

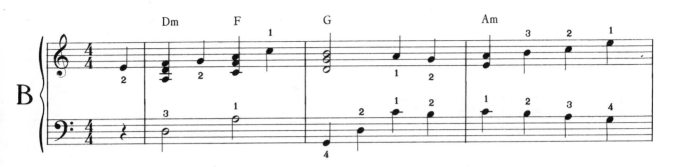

Bridal March from Lohengrin
(Here Comes The Bride)

Majestically

music by Richard Wagner

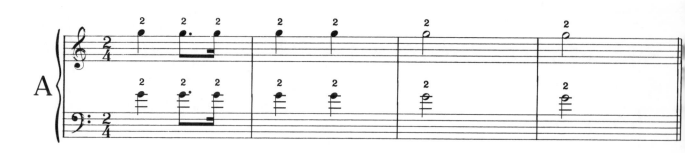

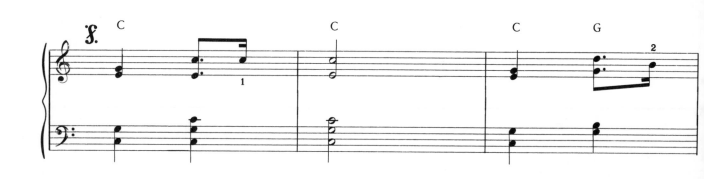

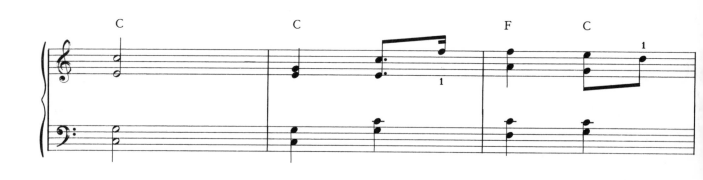

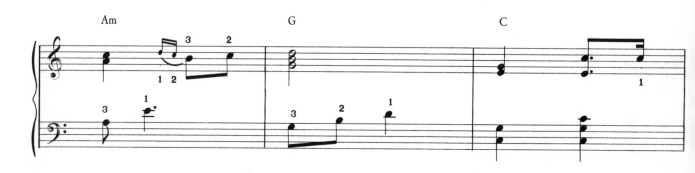

Bridal March from Lohengrin
(Here Comes The Bride)

Majestically

music by Richard Wagner

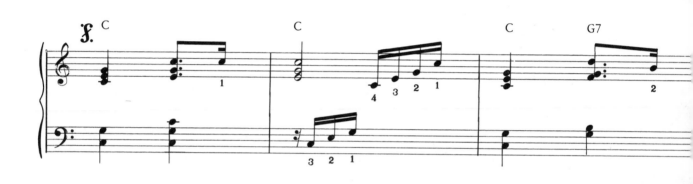

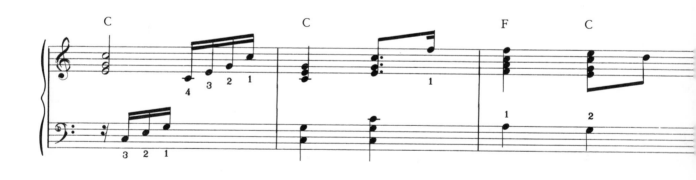

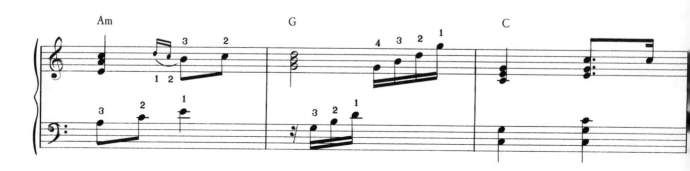

69

Trumpet Tune

Folk Harpers: Set the F above middle C as an F sharp, and the F below middle C as an F natural. These will not change throughout the piece. The F at the top of the treble staff will change as indicated in the 7th and 8th measures.

Majestically

music by Henry Purcell

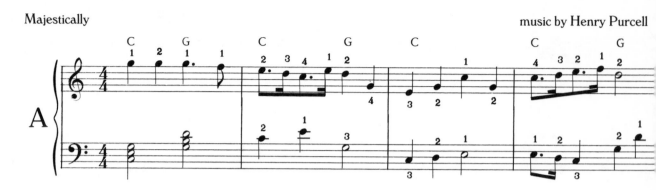

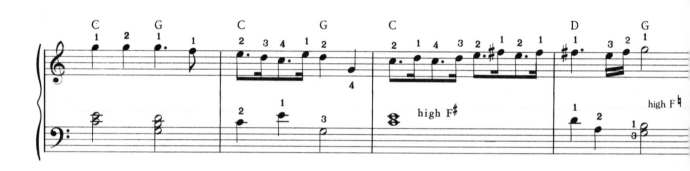

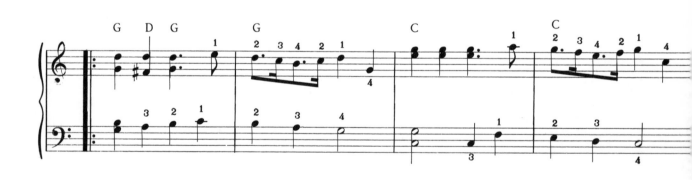

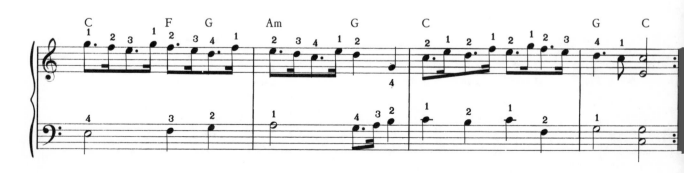

Trumpet Tune

Folk Harpers: Set the F above middle C as an F sharp, and the F below middle C as an F natural. These will not change throughout the piece. The F at the top of the treble staff will change as indicated in the 7th and 8th measures.

Majestically

music by Henry Purcell

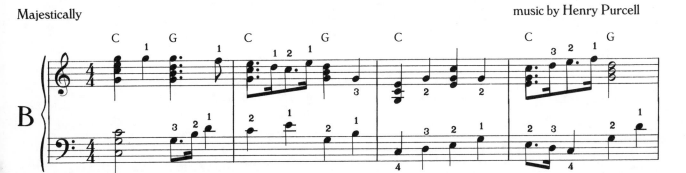

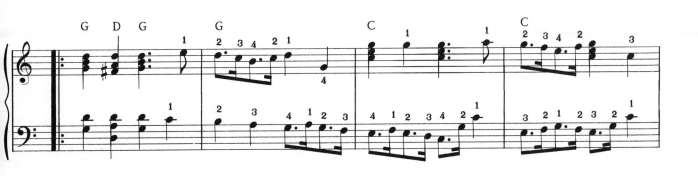

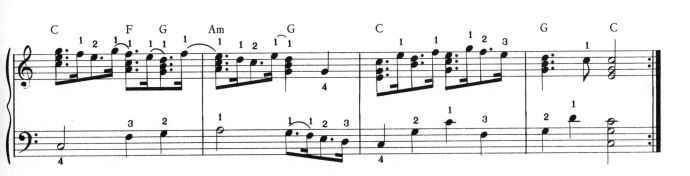

Trumpet Voluntary

Majestically

music by Henry Purcell

72

Trumpet Voluntary

Majestically

music by Henry Purcell

Artsa Alinu

Joyfully

traditional Israeli

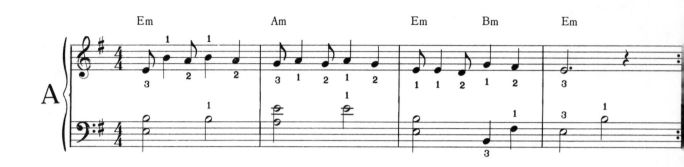

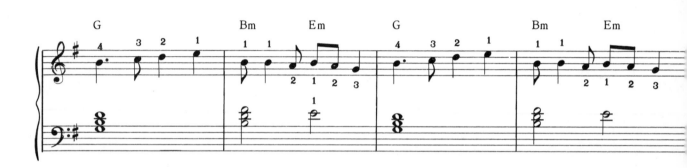

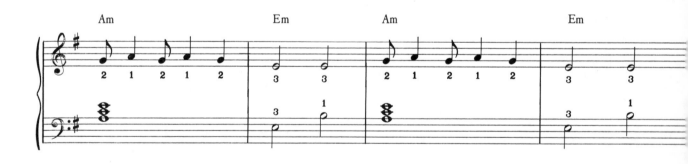

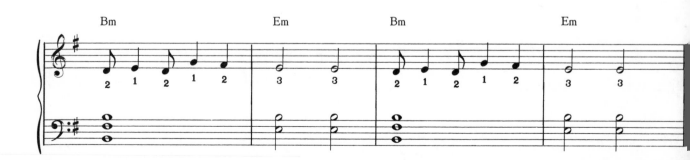

Artsa Alinu

Joyfully

traditional Israeli

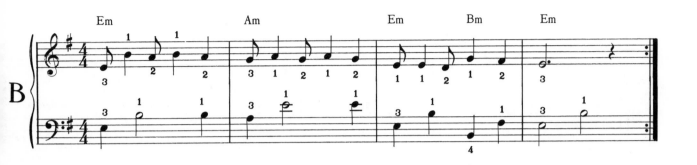

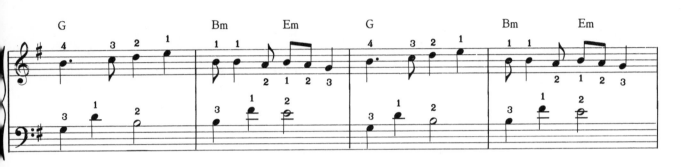

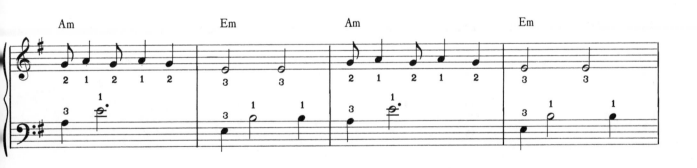

Hava Nagila

Folk Harpers: Sharp the G above middle C and the G below middle C before you begin. These will not change throughout the piece.

Joyfully

traditional Hassidic

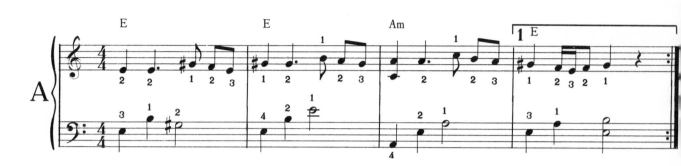

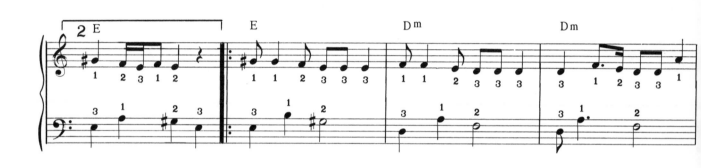

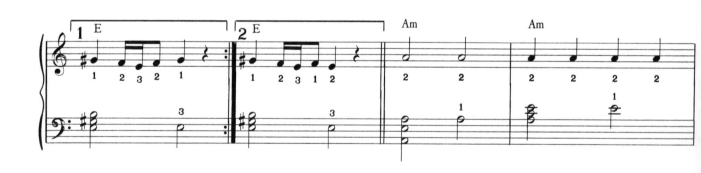

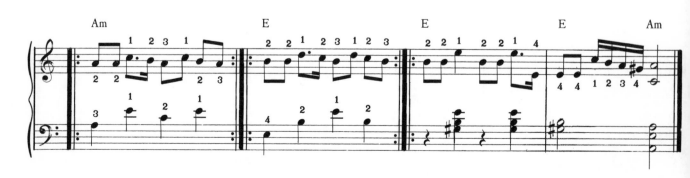

76

Hava Nagila

Folk Harpers: Sharp the G above middle C and the G below middle C before you begin. These will not change throughout the piece.

Joyfully   traditional Hassidic

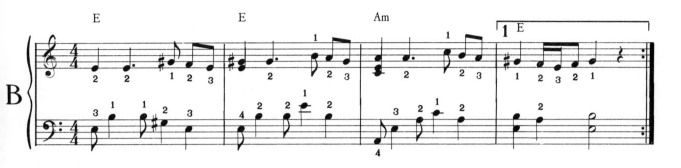

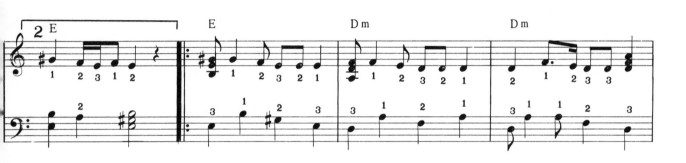

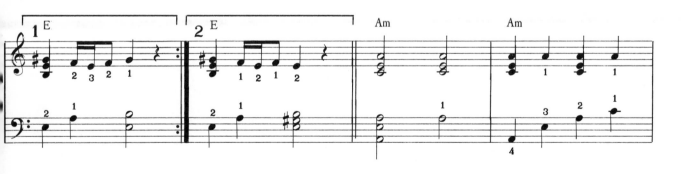

Hevenu Shalom

Joyfully

traditional Israeli

Hevenu Shalom

Folk Harpers: Set the D above middle C as a D sharp. It will not change throughout the piece. (B version only)

Joyfully

traditional Israeli

Hine Ma Tov #1

Moderately

traditional Israeli round

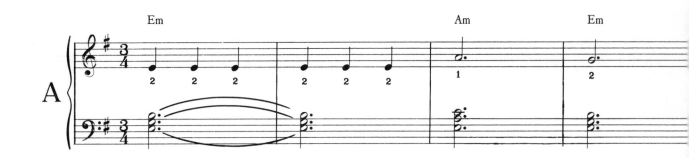

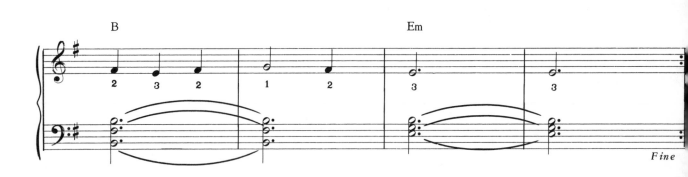

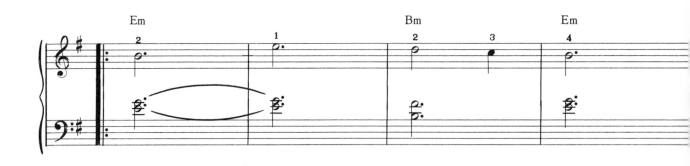

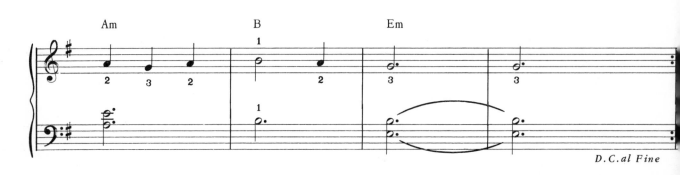

Hine Ma Tov #1

Moderately

traditional Israeli round

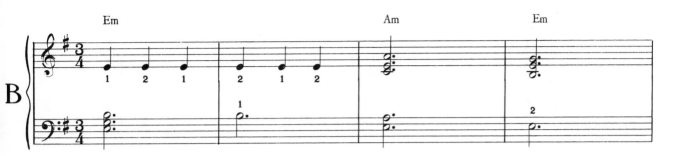

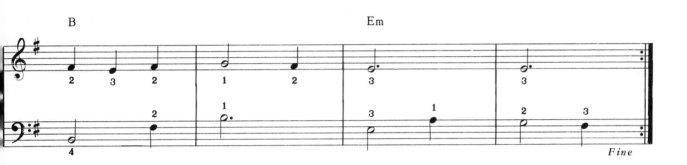

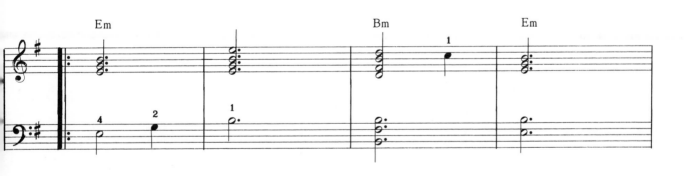

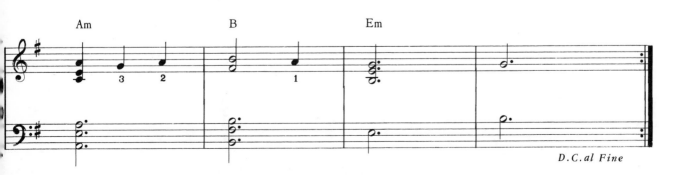

Hine Ma Tov #2

Folk Harpers: Set middle C as a C sharp, and the C below middle C as a C natural. They will not change throughout the piece.

Moderately

traditional Israeli

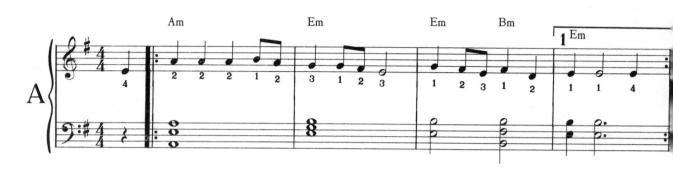

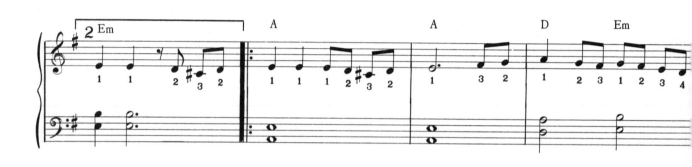

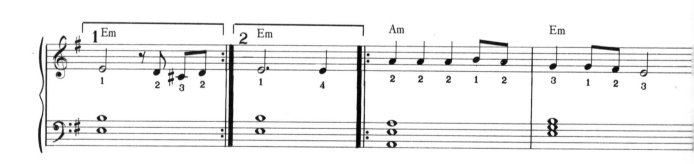

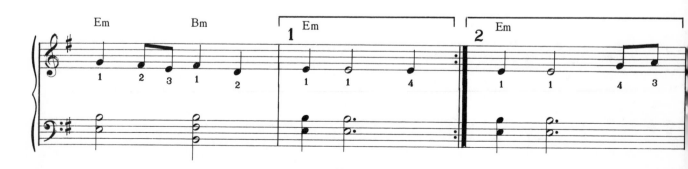

Hine Ma Tov #2

Folk Harpers: Set middle C as a C sharp, and the C below middle C as a C natural. They will not change throughout the piece.

Moderately

traditional Israeli

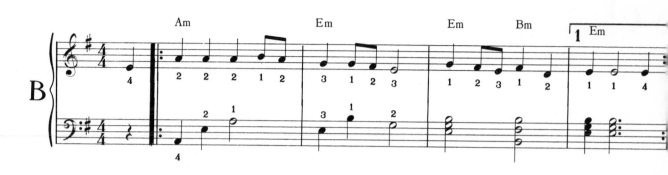

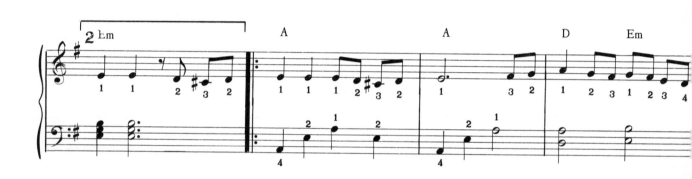

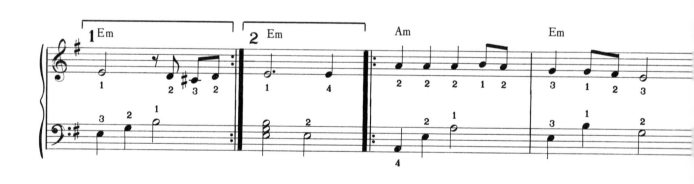

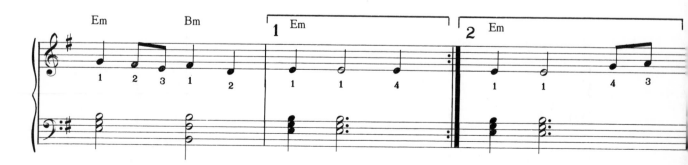

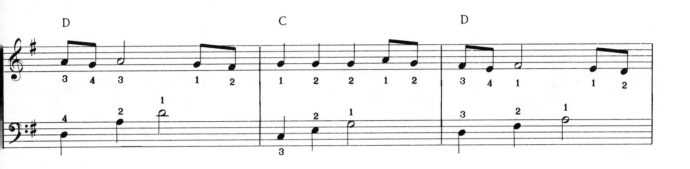

Kozatzke

Folk Harpers: Set the F an-octave-and-a-half above middle C as an F natural. It will not change throughout the piece.

Joyfully

traditional Israeli

Kozatzke

Folk Harpers: Set the F an-octave-and-a-half above middle C as an F natural. It will not change throughout the piece.

traditional Israeli

Joyfully

L'cha Dodi

Moderately

traditional Israeli

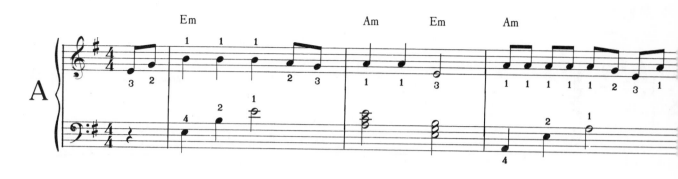

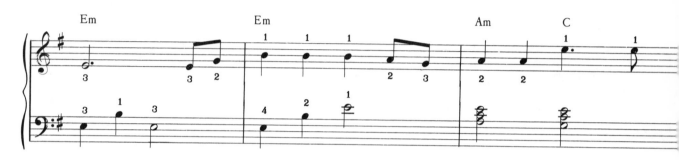

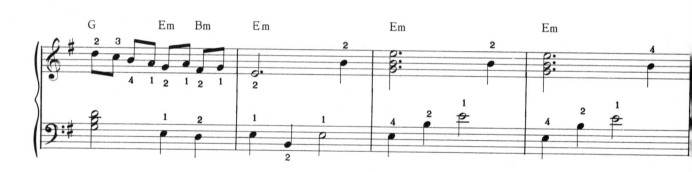

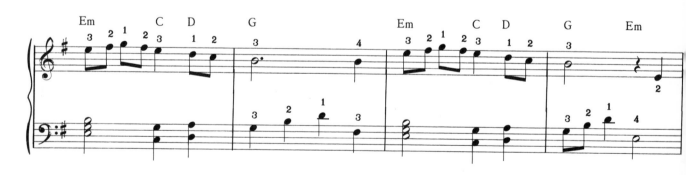

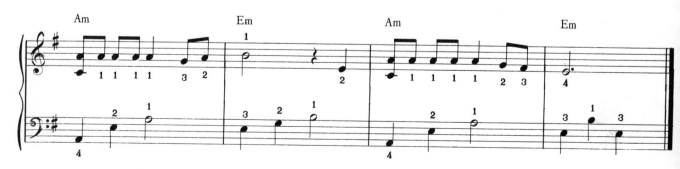

88

L'cha Dodi

Moderately

traditional Israeli

Ave Maria
Harp Part and Score

Slowly with feeling

adapted from music by Franz Schubert

Folk harpers: The F 1½ octaves above middle C should be set as an F natural, and will not change throughout the piece. Other accidentals are notated as follows: the C and D an octave below middle C are called "low C" and "low D", and the ones an octave above middle C are called "high C" and "high D". During most of this piece the left hand plays only on the down-beat. But when lever changes need to be made the right hand may take the whole measure. Notes with the stems up are for the right hand; stems down are for the left.

Once the melody begins, it is written on the top staff of each brace, and the harp part is written on the bottom two staves. The melody must be sung or played by a soloist: it is not included in the harp part.

Ben - e - di - cta tu in mu - li - e - ri - bus,

middle C♮

et be - ne - di - ctus,

et be - ne - dic - tus fru - ctus ven - tris,

low D♯

ven - tris tu - i Je - sus.

low D♮   low C♯

A - - - ve Ma - ri - - - - - a!

Ave Maria
Vocal or Instrumental Part

Slowly with feeling

adapted from music by Franz Schubert

OTHER MUSIC BOOKS BY SYLVIA WOODS

TEACH YOURSELF TO PLAY THE FOLK HARP

TEACH YOURSELF TO PLAY THE FOLK HARP teaches the student step by step how to play the folk harp. Each of the 12 lessons includes instructions, exercises, and folk and classical pieces using the new skills and techniques taught in the lesson. It is an excellent book for any student, regardless of previous musical training. 80 pages. Companion audio cassette also available.
A VIDEO companion to the TEACH YOURSELF TO PLAY THE FOLK HARP book is now available. On this informative video, Sylvia Woods demonstrates the pieces from the book, lesson by lesson, giving helpful hints and instruction as she plays. 1 hour 40 minutes long in VHS or Beta format.

SONGS OF THE HARP: 20 SONGS ABOUT HARPS AND HARPERS

SONGS OF THE HARP includes 20 songs dealing with harps and harpers. All of the harp arrangements include the melody, and therefore can be played with or without the vocal line. 48 pages.

IRISH DANCE TUNES FOR ALL HARPS: 50 Jigs, Reels, Hornpipes and Airs

This book contains 50 Irish jigs, reels, hornpipes and airs arranged for the harp. Each arrangement also includes chord symbols for harpers or other instrumentalists. This is an excellent book for harpers interested in learning about Irish dance tunes, or for those already involved in the Irish music scene. It can also be used by groups of musicians as well as harp soloists. 64 pages.

50 CHRISTMAS CAROLS FOR ALL HARPS: Each arranged for beginning and advanced harpers

This is the first book in the SYLVIA WOODS MULTI-LEVEL HARP BOOK SERIES: books designed to be used by harpers and harpists at all levels of proficiency. Each carol has two arrangements: an easy version, and one that is more difficult. Also, each carol contains the lyrics and chord indications that can be used by harpers or other instrumentalists. The two arrangements can be played as a duet. 96 pages spiral bound.

40 O'CAROLAN TUNES FOR ALL HARPS: Each arranged for beginning and advanced harpers

This is the second book in the SYLVIA WOODS MULTI-LEVEL HARP BOOK SERIES. The book contains 40 of the best tunes by O'Carolan, the most famous of the Irish harpers and composers who lived from 1670-1738. Each of the 40 tunes has two arrangements: an easy version, and one that is more difficult. Also, each tune includes chord indications that can be used by harpers or other instrumentalists. 112 pages spiral-bound.

MUSIC THEORY AND ARRANGING TECHNIQUES FOR FOLK HARPS

This book teaches harpers, step by step, the music theory and techniques they need to make their own arrangements. Subjects covered include chords, inversions, keys, accompaniment patterns, transposing, and much more. The book gives plenty of examples and includes more than 90 pieces on which the student can practice their newly gained skills as they progress through the book. 112 pages spiral-bound.

THE HARP OF BRANDISWHIERE

This book goes with Sylvia Woods' album of the same name. It contains the full story of the legend, beautifully illustrated by the English artist, Steve Duglas. It also includes the written music of the suite, which can be played on Celtic or pedal harp, or piano. For more information, see listing under "Albums and Cassettes". 60 pages.

CANON by PACHELBEL

Sylvia Woods has included several arrangements of this popular piece in this book, including: an easy solo version, advanced solo versions in the keys of G and D, a duet version for 2 harps, and an arrangement for harp and melody instrument. 26 pages spiral-bound.

ALBUMS AND CASSETTES BY SYLVIA WOODS

THE HARP OF BRANDISWHIERE

THE HARP OF BRANDISWHIERE is the highly acclaimed Suite for Celtic Harp by SYLVIA WOODS. Sylvia's beautiful compositions musically present the fantasy story of Brandiswhiere, the magical harper of legend. Sylvia plays both nylon-strung and metal-strung Celtic harps, and is accompanied by acoustic instruments such as flutes, trumpets, cimbalom, celeste, acoustic bass, and percussion. The music is all instrumental, with no singing or speaking, and the instruments weave a fine and intricate aural tapestry to illustrate the legend. THE HARP OF BRANDISWHIERE book (sold separately) contains the full story of the legend, beautifully illustrated by the English artist, Steve Duglas. It also includes the written music of the suite, which can be played on Celtic or pedal harp, or piano. Album, cassette, or book.

THREE HARPS FOR CHRISTMAS

What better way to enhance the festive mood of your holidays than with this fine collection of traditional Christmas carols? Drawn from many countries, and recorded by world-renowned folk harper Sylvia Woods, these lovely arrangements are performed on three special harps: the nylon-strung Neo-Celtic harp, the metal-strung Ancient Celtic harp, and the rare triple-strung harp. Each carol is performed by Sylvia on one, two, or three harps, with no other accompaniment. The recording includes 28 carols, including most of your favorites. This beautiful album is a perfect gift for yourself and anyone on your Christmas list. Album or cassette.

Alphabetical Index Of Tunes